Praise for
Flying Lessons

I think this book should be included with any baby book as a gift to new moms. That way she'll know what to do to in order to achieve the end result...an enduring connection with her grown son. – *Chris S.*

Your son needs you to read this book. – *David V.*

Lauren includes an incredibly informative chapter on hormones (both hers and her son's) and menopause. That part alone is worth the price of admission! – *Susan W.*

A wonderful read. You will enjoy and learn from this book describing a life filled with love between a mother and her son. – *Steve C.*

Don't wait until your child is approaching the age of separation; read this book NOW so you can help create the adult human you have dreamed of. Fun and light reading with a lot of powerful messages. – *Jana R.*

A must read for any woman raising boys. Thank you, Lauren, for this gift. – *Andre P.*

If you have a teen or twenty something son, you need to read this book. It explains so much about what your son will be going through and helps you to understand how to support them as they spread their wings and fly. - *Terry T.*

This is well written and if you have an adolescent or teenager, son in particular, I think you will appreciate this book and be glad you read it. – *Christina E.*

My son will be 18 in a few months so I'm feeling all the emotions that come with that. This book was right on time for me. - *Jennifer*

I love this book! There is bittersweet sadness to this story, yet this book with all its humor makes their flying away almost feel magical. I love that the author shares her story, her knowledge and her practical wisdom while using the wonderfully sweet comparison of the mama bird watching her little bird flying away from the nest. – *Jodi L.*

DOWNLOAD YOUR FREE *FLYING LESSONS* JOURNAL—YOUR QUIET PLACE TO REFLECT AND REALIGN, ONE PAGE AT A TIME—BECAUSE WRITING THINGS DOWN IS HOW YOU FIND YOUR WAY THROUGH.

authorjoy.com/journal

Flying LESSONS

Empty Nesting for Single Boy Moms

— New 2nd Edition —

LAUREN JOHNSON

Copyright © 2026 by Lauren Johnson

lauren@authorjoy.com

All rights reserved. No part of this publication may be reproduced, stored in a retrieval system, or transmitted, in any form or by any means without the prior written permission of the publisher, nor be otherwise circulated in any form of binding or cover other than that in which it is published and without a similar condition being imposed on the subsequent purchaser.

The author of this book does not dispense medical advice or prescribe the use of any technique as a form of treatment for physical, emotional, or medical problems without the advice of a physician, either directly or indirectly. The intent of the author is only to offer information of a general nature to help you in your quest for emotional and hormonal well-being. In the event you use any of the information in this book for yourself, the author and the publisher assume no responsibility for your actions.

ISBN: 978-1-7327436-3-2 (Paperback)
ISBN: 978-1-7327436-1-8 (E-book)
ISBN: 978-1-7327436-2-5 (Audiobook)

FAMILY & RELATIONSHIPS / Parenting / Single Parent
BODY, MIND & SPIRIT / Inspiration & Personal Growth
BIOGRAPHY & AUTOBIOGRAPHY / Memoirs

Second Edition

Printed in the United States of America
Published by Author Joy, LLC, Spearfish, South Dakota

Dedication

For Everett

My greatest teacher

Contents

PRAISE FOR FLYING LESSONS i
DEDICATION v
INTRODUCTION ix

CHAPTER ONE
The Amazing Stages of Your Son's Development 1

CHAPTER TWO
How to Communicate with Your Son as a Growing
Young Man 14

CHAPTER THREE
Hormones: His and Yours 29

CHAPTER FOUR
Seek Wise Counsel from Trusted Men 42

CHAPTER FIVE
Pre-flight Preparation for You 59

CHAPTER SIX
Pre-flight Preparation for Your Son 83

CHAPTER SEVEN
Vulnerability: His and Yours 101

CHAPTER EIGHT
Create "Completion" with Your Child 115

CHAPTER NINE
Ten Signs You're a Good Mom 126

CHAPTER TEN
Take Off 134

AFTERWORD 145
RECOMMENDED RESOURCES 147

Introduction

My nineteen-year-old son threw his body across the foot of my bed as I planned the next day's to-do list. This was the last night Everett and I were going to live together. Tomorrow I was moving out of our two-bedroom condo. It was empty nesting in reverse—instead of his being pushed from the nest, it was I who pushed myself. After fifteen years as a single mom and thirteen years of a difficult marriage before that, I needed to live alone. I took a job as a property manager to help a friend turn her two-million-dollar estate into a vacation rental on VRBO.com. The home was on five acres in a ritzy part of Louisville, and I was to live in the carriage house across from the historic home. It had been a longtime dream to live in a tiny house in the country yet somehow also in the city, and the opportunity fell in my lap.

"What are you doing, mom?" he said.

"Trying to decide what to do next. How to arrange the furniture. How to do the Feng Shui. Stuff like that."

He stretched his long, lean body across my papers and magazines and pretended to yawn, landing squarely in the middle of my bed and placing his cheek on his forearm.

INTRODUCTION

"Can I help you?" I said.

He popped up his head. "No, your bed's just comfortable," he said while stretching his arms even more to further cover the notebooks and magazines strewn across my bed.

After a moment, I asked, "Wanna see my plans?"

"Not really," he said.

He lingered a while. We chatted a bit. It didn't really matter what about.

And just as quickly and deliberately as he threw himself on the bed, he sat up and said, "Ok, this was fun. I'm going back to my room now. Love you, *mom*."

And off he went. Emphasizing my mom title was one of his ways of labeling and elevating me at the same time. That along with *mommy* and *mother*, depending on his mood.

I was going to miss him. I had no idea how much at the time, but I knew this was a special moment I'd never forget. This was our last official night to live together. You never know what a momentous occasion that is until you never have one like it again.

A few days later, I was unpacking boxes in the garage underneath the carriage house, surrounded by the lush, wooded property that abutted beautiful Cherokee Park to my right. An original owner of the estate, Frederick Law Olmsted, was commissioned to design a park system for Louisville in 1891 that highlighted the topography unique to each sector of the city. He designed a system of interconnecting parkways to link them. I was excited about living on this magnificent property while endeavoring to launch my book writing career and live serenely on my own.

Suddenly, a baby bird flew in through one of the open garage doors and scrambled to land somewhere…anywhere. It flew toward one of the windows, grasping frantically, chirping wildly. It finally gave up and managed to land on one of the chains of the garage door opener. It perched a while, noticeably shaken. Its wings were fluffed and puffy, and it teetered a bit as it wondered what to do next.

"It's okay," I said in what I thought was a very encouraging voice. "You're going to be fine. It's going to be okay."

It blinked at me, not quite ready to try taking off again.

"Really, it's okay. You'll be fine. No one's going to hurt you. Just fly out the door. Fly that way."

I pointed toward the open door and the trees outside. I sounded like a crazy lady. A kind and helpful one, but crazy, nonetheless.

My words didn't work, so I decided to inch toward the bird with the hope that it would take flight. Its parents were chirping madly on a nearby tree as if to say, "Come this way. Do it this way. Don't get near strangers." As I moved closer, it took off but made a wrong turn and landed on a windowsill. I moved closer again, trying to help it turn toward the opening, turning back toward its freedom. And this time it did. The baby bird took off with great ceremony, out into the world, and landed on a nearby tree.

I thought at the time of the irony. Here I was, embarking on my new life, just like that bird. I wasn't sure how I was going to do it or how it would turn out, but I was sure as hell flapping my wings, even if it did look like simply emptying boxes.

Inside one box was a Mother's Day present Everett had given me when he was about 10 years old—a Star Wars Y-Wing fighter made of mostly grey and white Legos. As I carefully held it up and turned it from side to side, admiring his handiwork and

INTRODUCTION

remembering the loving smile on his face when he gave it to me, I started to cry.

And then those simple tears turned into something loud and gulping with wrenching sobs. My tears mixed with the dust from the boxes, so I soon had grimy lines of brown grit running all over my face. Wiping my face with my dusty sleeves helped nothing. I was all alone, in a garage, on a gorgeous estate, feeling things I had never felt before. I was one big mess running into the house with the Y-wing in my hand. I gently placed it on the dresser and threw myself on my bed, where I remained for about an hour with intermittent sobbing.

This wasn't going to be as easy as I thought.

In fact, this was to be the first of many such crying jags to follow in the months ahead. Empty nesting was not going to be the full-fledged fling into freedom that I thought it would be.

When Everett was approaching puberty, I began daydreaming about what it was going to be like to be free from early wake-up calls to drive him to school, juggling a full-time career and single motherhood, feeding him every day and night, endless grocery shopping, endless emergency errands for things like poster boards and colored pencils, and all the piles of his clean clothes that covered the dryer in the laundry room. I pictured the joy of dancing without his saying, "Mom, stop dancing!" as he walked toward the kitchen. I imagined it would be like me in my twenties when I left my parents' home for the first time and had my own apartment. I saw myself being able to undress without closing my door and other niceties like the smell of candles wafting in the living room while I quietly read books and drank a glass of champagne. It was going to be heaven.

This was not to be the case.

FLYING LESSONS

Flying Lessons details the bittersweet truth that single moms must actually learn to fly just as much as their young ones. Transformation requires the courage to step outside of what's safe and step into a place where you end up having more questions than answers. It's an epic paradigm shift away from the construct in which you lived.

This book is set up to help you move out of the old paradigm and into the new. I hope the experiences, practices, and lessons I share in this book will help you work through your own transformation from parenting to post-parenting with joy, humor, and love. It is true that our babies will always be our babies, we just have to learn how to stop treating them that way.

Using personal stories, cutting edge research on parenting adult sons, expert advice, and methods for creating a new relationship with your son, you'll be able to discover your own path while your child discovers his. *Flying Lessons* will help you navigate the challenging transition that comes after years of being a single mom. You'll both be able to take flight with preparation, planning, expecting the unexpected, and, with practice, spreading your wings.

A week or so after my son's and my separation, he visited me for dinner. He probably did so more for the mom-cooked meal than the company of mom herself.

But that didn't matter. He was there, and he'd been living his own transformation day by day. He looked *older*.

"Mom," he said, looking down at the plate of spaghetti and picking up his fork. "There is nothing that should be more respected than a single mom." He took a bite. "At least the good ones, that is."

INTRODUCTION

I paused, not knowing if I should ask the obvious. But I couldn't help myself.

"Do you include me in that category?"

"Yes," he said while shoving another forkful of spaghetti into his mouth. "And thank you for that."

CHAPTER ONE

The Amazing Stages of Your Son's Development

In the age of Camelot, a man's life was characterized by four distinct stages: page, knight, prince, and king. All a page wanted was to be a knight with a horse. In modern times, all a page wants to be is a knight with a car. Alison Armstrong, author of numerous books about men and founder of www.understandmen.com, identified these stages for modern men as a guideline for understanding them throughout their lives. Men are always looking to move to the next stage of manhood. At the same time a mom is going through the process of empty nesting, her son is going through the process of becoming a knight.

Armstrong says that knighthood begins at puberty and lasts until the late twenties. Their lives are characterized by an intense need for adventure. Knights are driven by fun, challenge, conquest, and speed—none of which necessarily includes a mom.

UNDERSTAND YOUR KNIGHT

Knights put up boundaries

As a knight, your son's sense of self is evolving. Before high school ends, he begins the process of separating from you. Boundaries are drawn *by him*. Oftentimes, it feels like your son is raising the drawbridge to the castle, and you're standing on the other side of the moat wanting to holler, "*Wait!*"

I'll never forget the time when my son was 17 and getting ready for bed. It was a night like any other, and he emerged from his bedroom to brush his teeth and kiss me goodnight. However, this time he announced, "Mom, I've decided I don't want to kiss you good night anymore."

Someone pull the stake out of my heart.

His words left me with a thick lump in my throat. No words of mine could explain what I felt or change the outcome of his decision. So, I said, in what I hope did not reveal the tears I would be shedding later, "Okay."

My son was making decisions based on his need to grow into manhood. As a single mom, I needed to honor what he needed and support him during this time of rapid growth. You will be forced to reckon with the same.

"We now know that a male's primary job starting around age 12, in order for him to find himself and build his character, is to get away from his mother," says Andre Paradis, relationship coach, NLP coach, workshop leader, and the author of *Purpose, Passion, and Profit*. "In order for him to become a good man, that is what he must do." Andre says that this is the time for women to stop mothering their sons. "That means you don't wake him up in the morning to take the bus. You let him wake himself up. And if he misses the bus, it's on him.

"It's not what many moms want to hear, but you must let go of control," Andre says. "If you make rules around him that keep him from thinking for himself and doing for himself, you are stunting his necessary growth as a man. You must put control of his life back on him. If you overprotect him, over baby him, over mother him, he can't find his way. And he becomes one of those guys who never grows up. We have plenty of examples of these guys out there right now."

Knights live for fun

One late Saturday morning when Everett was a senior in high school, he went to the kitchen to pour a bowl of cereal. He then walked out with a half-full bowl and said, "Yo Yo, Ma. We ain't got no cereal, cuz."

"Huh? I just bought some yesterday."

I went to the cupboard to grab the remaining box of cereal— the one that was "mine" as opposed to "his." When I shook it, there was nothing inside.

I looked at Everett, holding up the box.

"Why must you put an empty box back in the cupboard?"

"To see that look on your face right now," he said, and grinned after he spooned in a big bite.

I tried to stifle my laugh to no avail.

When your son chooses what's fun for him, it's not wise or helpful to diminish his choice or scold him for it. He's doing what's *normal* for him. In her DVD, *The Amazing Development of Men* (PAX Programs, 2008), Alison Armstrong says, "When my son chose fun, I didn't lose respect for him or think that I had done something wrong as a mother or that I didn't instill responsibility. Instead, I knew the way to support and love him was to be his taxi driver."

You want to have faith in what you have already done to bring him to this point in his life. You want him to feel safe to not only have fun, but for him to tell you about it, too. Fun is not about doing anything bad or wrong, though fun can often include making mistakes. That's just who he is and what he's going to do. That's how he learns about life.

"I'm the parent who built the zipline in the backyard," says Laura Bartlett, single mom of two sons and comedian, entrepreneur, executive producer of *Four Funny Females,* and founder of HospitalHostageHelp.com. "I knew that my youngest son had this real adventurous streak in him, and I just really wanted to nurture it. I don't know if I necessarily wanted to push him out of a moving car saying, 'Y'know, this'll really get you up to speed son.' I just didn't want to stifle his need for adventure. I wanted to celebrate it and his uniqueness.

"It was a very hard decision at times," Laura says. "But I don't regret any of the nights I stood outside holding a flashlight in the pitch dark while my son did tricks over ramps to ramps while his friend lied down on the ground and my son jumped over him. I didn't mind being the person to hold the flashlight. I know there were parents wondering, 'Why are they out there doing that? Why aren't they inside going to bed?'"

Want to be the kind of mom your knight needs? Then be the mom who doesn't try to stop, control, or diminish his choices. Don't be the mom who wants to drum it into him that he must choose other things over fun. Your son will withdraw *from you*, not the fun. Boys in the knight stage are very passionate about living. If he's saving money, there's a good chance he's saving it for his next adventure, however he defines it.

I heard a mom on a radio show talking about how much she missed her son's playfulness. She sounded quite sad about it. The host asked, "How long has he been gone?" The mom said, "Two years."

Knights are compelled to leave the nest

As a mom, you have the opportunity to provide a safe place for your son to rest and refuel, as long as you don't pummel him with questions like, "What did you do?" and "Where did you go?" If you have the willingness to provide that pitstop, and if you do so happily without nagging, complaint, or the expectation of control, you're going to be able to create a lifelong relationship with your son where he still wants to come back home to see you, no matter how old he is.

Talking about her own son, Alison Armstrong says he wasn't *choosing* to leave, he was *compelled* to leave.

"There was nothing more to learn at home about life for him," she says. "If he was going to succeed, if he was going to survive, then he had to leave to learn these things. He had to go out into the world and conquer."

Don't take it personally that he doesn't want to stay home. "Our species is one of the few that keeps its young studs," Armstrong says. "In most species, they're driven from the herd to go hang with their peers." Just like birds.

One afternoon early in his senior year, Everett came home from school and said, "Hey mom, can I go to the mall to meet some friends?"

"You mean, you would rather go to the mall than stay here and spend quality time with your mother?" I said.

"You mean, the quality time that I love so much?" he said.

"Yes."

"I'd rather go to the mall."

Knights live in the present

Young knights are rarely preparing for what they want to do next or for when they grow up. For example, my son was fortunate to receive an inheritance from one of my sisters when he was about 20. Even though he knew that she wanted him to be happy, he also knew that she wanted him to use that money for college. Suddenly, he had this overwhelming need to buy some type of thousand-dollar bike. He was looking at pictures and figuring out what kind of seat it should have and the best trim for the wheels. It was so funny because I'd not seen him show any interest in bicycling since he was around 13!

My choice would have been to put that check in the bank and keep it there for school. I had to remind myself, *this is ok. This is his money. My sister wanted him to be happy.* The only thing I could do was offer some awareness. As long as he understood the financial impact of the decision he was making, the choice was his to make. It's our job as moms to bite our tongues when it comes to their choices.

Knight energy can lift you up

"As women and moms, when we get older, we get so serious," Armstrong says. "We need that knight energy to lighten us up, bring us back to the present, pull us away from our multi-tasking, and engage us in something that demands our full attention and participation, *just because*."

When your son comes home with boundless energy, notice how fun he is and listen to the passion with which he shares his stories with you. If you allow him to do that and allow yourself to take in his exuberance, you are going to feel the same possibility for yourself. Let his energy feed your soul. He has plenty to go around.

On one particularly stressful day for me, my son asked me to drive him somewhere. I remember begrudgingly hopping in the car, feeling as if another task had just been added to my already long list for the evening. He had me take a side road through one of the city's gorgeous parks as a shortcut. He pointed out some of his favorite spots as we drove through the winding park road. As we approached a turn, he told me to slow down and look to the left. "Look, mom. Right there. The best swing in the city." He was right. It was a solo swing in a private spot that was surrounded by trees.

"Do you still swing?" I asked.

"Whenever there's a good one," he said.

If you're a safe place for them to share their adventures, their passion will be contagious. I went back to that spot to swing the next day.

Knights may not be "ready"

During the knight phase, you might hear the words, "I'm not ready." What he's telling you is literal. What that usually means for a knight is that he hasn't done everything he wants to do before committing to something new.

"Readiness is a state of being for a man which means that, in his mind, in his world, he has what it takes to be successful in his choices," Armstrong says. "He feels he's mature enough, responsible enough, has the resources, and has the space to commit."

It's not your job to make him be ready, or convince him to be ready, or to tell him all the reasons he should be ready. That job is over. It's his life, and it's his time to take possession of it. That's a key stage of his development. It's up to him to know when he's ready, not you.

"One of the most important things I did was to take the time to help my sons find their purpose," says Laura. "And I really pat myself on the back for doing that."

Neither of Laura's sons went to college. Laura recognized early on that her oldest son, Charlie, was the computer guy. "I let him crash a lot of my computers," she said. "He'd put a bunch of viruses on my computer early on. I survived that, so I figured that's probably what he should do for life. He's now a sought-after and self-taught software engineer in New York City."

Laura remembers when her youngest son didn't quite know the path he was heading toward after high school. He wanted to be an entrepreneur but didn't know how or what to do. "So, he had a little bit of growing up to do, because he just didn't know," Laura says. "What I'm proud of doing is that I didn't just push him out the door anyway. If your child has to work to just survive and pay bills, then they don't have time to think about what their purpose is."

Laura didn't want her sons to have to muddle through a bunch of shitty jobs just to pay rent. "I wanted them to be who they were meant to be, not made in my or society's image." Laura tells the story of sitting with her son at Starbucks when he was about 20 years old. Her son had been working hard as a mechanic for a while, but to her (and her son) it was just a placeholder. "We were looking out the window, and he kind of threw up his hands and just said, 'I don't know what I'm supposed to do. I feel lost.'"

Laura told him, "You're not. Let me help you. As your GPS, you're in the sitting section of Starbucks. I kind of know you, I think, and maybe better than you know yourself." She explained that he might be too close to the subject matter to see clearly. "You have always loved doing mechanical things. You've taken your skateboards apart. You've taken your bikes apart. You've taken your scooters apart. You've been an adrenaline junky. You've cliff dived. If you could've skydived, you would've done that. You've done trick skiing. You do all these daring and adventurous things. And they seem to have everything to do with speed."

She acknowledged his hard work as a mechanic. "But that's not your stopping point," she said. "That's just you understanding cars. What I really see you doing is being behind the wheel of the car. I see you as a race car driver."

Her son's demeanor immediately changed. He sat up and said, "Wow, I guess I never even thought that I could do this. Like, I didn't even know that was a possibility." Then Laura said, "I don't know how the hell it would happen either, but there isn't anyone

I'd rather be in a passenger seat with than you when going around a street pole drifting on an icy day in your Mazda Miata!"

Laura said it truly was zeroing in on what she knew about her son and not about the questions of 'can he make a living at this' or 'will he be successful?' "Those questions didn't pop in my mind," she said. "My questions were, 'Who is he? What makes him tick? Where does he get his mojo from?'"

Everett was not ready to begin college right after high school. I myself wasn't ready to begin college after high school. One year off served me very well as a time to work and save money and grow up. No one in my family pressured me to go to school. My parents knew me and knew I had a plan. They stepped back and allowed me the space to let it happen.

Everett, on the other hand, was bombarded with comments from friends or other family members that "the longer you stay out of school, the less likely you will ever go back." That's the fear or opinion of someone else projected onto you. In the time since Everett left high school, he worked his way from Wendy's, to Panera, to full-time server in a fine-dining restaurant. He's supported himself fully since age 21. He completed general studies and prerequisites at the local community college (just like his mom), and he is now completing his degree in finance at a four-year college. His sense of accomplishment and independence will feed his continued success at school and in life, knowing he did it his way.

One thing moms can do to support their sons in becoming "ready" is to ask these questions: "Can you help me understand what you want to accomplish before you're ready? What is it going to take for you to feel ready? What does ready look like for you?" And then give him time to answer.

Dr. Beth Halbert, owner of Compassionate Power Parenting and author of *Embracing Defiance*, concurs. "Ask your child what they want and need to know in order to feel like they're ready to be an adult," she said. "I did this with a parent one time and their son said, 'Well, I want to know how to cook that spaghetti dish, and I want to know how to wash clothes that are fragile.' This kid had like five or six things that the parent knew how to do, but the child hadn't learned yet."

Bruce Dane, an actuary and father of a daughter and two sons, also warns of having too many expectations for your kid. "You want them to achieve things. Where we live, I see a lot of pressure from other parents," he says. "But you need to be supportive of who they want to be, not who you think they should be. I certainly see a lot of parents around here like, 'Oh my God, what are you trying to do?' I say give your kid a little breathing room rather than regimenting everything."

Fred Miller, a rescue diver and widowed dad of a son and daughter, says, "Realize that you've given them the information, the guidance, the health development, the creed inside that enables them to separate from you and actually use what you taught them." Fred also cautions parents to be ready if plans change. "Realize there's trial and error, and the timing has to be just right *for them*. Let them know they have a place to return if things don't work out the first time, and then just do a re-do and try it again."

Terri Kendall, Psy.S, single mom of two daughters and author of *Be Your Best Self,* worked with students in the Jefferson County School District in Louisville, Kentucky for more than twenty years. "Sometimes there are reasons parents don't know of for why their son may not be ready," she says. "Parents ask questions like, 'Are they ADHD or are they just not doing the work? What's interfering with their grades dropping?' Sometimes, the answer is, 'I think they get high too much.'"

Terri sees two different camps that most seniors fall in. "Some say 'I just want to graduate from high school. I don't know what I'll do,'" says Terri. "Then others are like, 'No, I want to get into a good school. How do I get my grades up, and what do I do?'"

Terri has a friend with a son who is a senior in high school. "She's really pushing him to do college visits and submit applications. She said when she hears his friends, both male and female, say that they're not even looking toward the future yet, she thinks, 'Oh my gosh, we're not going to have that. I don't want to hear my son say, *I don't really know what I'm doing after high school.*'"

Show your knight you're "ready"

Sometimes, it's really the parent who's not ready. Dr. Beth Halbert says that "one of the things I would say to parents is that your kids are actually anxious that *you're* okay and *you're* ready, not as much that they are."

I had my first experience of feeling "not ready" shortly after Everett graduated from high school. His graduation gift was a four-day ticket to the annual Bonnaroo Music and Arts Festival in Manchester, Tennessee, which was a few hundred miles from home. This was to be his first trip with friends on his own. I was a nervous wreck as the day approached. And it didn't help when a male friend of mine gave Everett a new tent and sleeping bag. I said, "So, my son is going hundreds of miles away to a place with music, sex, and drugs, and you're giving him a bedroom to-go to make it all easy?!"

I posted my growing emotional meltdown on Facebook: "My kid is leaving today for a 4-day trip to Bonnaroo, which I guess is a lot like Woodstock except with less LSD and more porta-potties. It's his graduation gift, including a tent and sleeping bag. I'm thinking I should be afraid...very, very afraid."

My friends helped me with perspective. My beloved friend, Joanne, who was in the maternity room with me when Everett was born said, "I'd be more afraid if you and I were going." One male friend said, "Excellent! I've actually heard of and like 20% of the scheduled line-up." Another man said, "This sounds like a great opportunity to dialogue your parental concerns and tell him why you trust him to be a good self-manager." One mom said, "Of course you get to do the sad, scared thing. Then, when you have had quite enough, take yourself to dinner and celebrate the wonderful joy of having him be capable of such adventures. One without the other wouldn't be balanced." Another male friend said, "Ever see a baby bird fly well from the nest with the mother bird strapped to its back? Trust the job you've done just as he trusted what you taught him and honor his choices. It is, after all, his life."

Who knew Facebook could be such a source of wisdom? The next day, when I awoke and realized I had four days all to myself to do whatever I wanted, I posted: "Momma's gotta new pair of shoes!"

CHAPTER TWO
How to Communicate with Your Son as a Growing Young Man

I didn't believe Melissa, a friend and financial expert, when she told me in 2012 that I would become a champion for men. She experienced what I can only describe as a divine download when she shared with me the insights and images she had about my future. For about 30 minutes, I took notes as she said she saw me advocating for the welfare of sons and men. My intention had always been to be an advocate for girls. Even though Melissa's words were fascinating, they didn't ring true for me at the time.

Now they do.

I kept those notes, and this book expands my journey as a champion for men. My "why" is my son. It is also your son.

POST-MODERN MEN AND WOMEN

I'm one of the original champions of women. I had to be, given the era in which I grew up and the time I entered the business world. So did the women who went before me. American women are now quote unquote *empowered*. That job is done. American women are the most fortunate and powerful and free women on the planet, thanks to our founding fathers and mothers and the idea that all men and women are created equal. Institutionalized sexism against women no longer exists in our country. In fact, quite the opposite is true, as colleges and companies twist themselves in knots to increase participation by women and denigrate participation by men. Our culture and campuses and corporations now deliberately *exclude* men in order to have a more *inclusive* environment. The nonsense of that new way of being is just a blatant new form of institutionalized sexism. Women don't win by causing men to fail.

There are many books and resources from authors and social scientists who are more experienced than I in writing about this topic. For now, this chapter serves as a rallying cry for moms, daughters, and sisters to stop persecuting men. Men are of equal value to women and vice versa. I thought that lesson had been learned a long time ago.

Today's culture is demonizing white men

The anti-male narrative that has seized the dominant culture is dangerous and disturbing. Colleges and the media have robbed men of their due process (though that has been legally restored on college campuses as of 2025). College professors dismiss young men's raised hands, even when no female students in the room are raising theirs. Angry women scream "patriarchy" as being some modern-day problem and antithesis to decency and law and order. It is the so-called American patriarchy that created the space for women to be free, equal, and heard in the first place.

My son now has a target on him for simply being a white male, as if he has something to apologize for because of existing with immutable characteristics. I'm thankful he's not yet an "old white man" because our culture deems them as having some sort of an inherent mental incapacity. My hope is that we can course correct before the sexism and hatred toward anyone's son's existence threatens their ability to be happy and productive in the world.

The statistics aren't good. One study shows that about 35% of young men in their twenties think that asking a woman out for a drink is sexual harassment. Men have become fearful of mentoring women in the workplace due to the sheer power of a woman's false allegations. The mortality rate of American men is declining. Their participation in the labor force is shrinking. Alcohol and drug addiction are soaring as is male suicide. Men are far more likely than women to drop out of high school, not go to college, go to jail, and die of a drug overdose, yet the problem is being ignored.

Men are being falsely accused, while women are supposed to be "believed" simply because of their gender. In fact, if you were to listen to the pundits and policy leaders, you'd think men are *too* successful and therefore must choose to step aside or be forced to do so. Nonsensical phrases like "toxic masculinity" and "male privilege" have been bandied about for over a decade as if they actually mean something. They don't, and they never did. In 2026, there are many signs that the trends to undermine men (especially white men) are lessening. What I find laughable is a certain political party spending $20 million on a study following the 2024 presidential election to find out how to speak to young men!

Everyone has a father, husband, brother, uncle, boyfriend, grandfather, partner, or colleague who is being told by society that he is bad, wrong, and a problem to be fixed. In the dominant culture, one gender's success now requires the other gender to be forced backward. I doubt there are many moms who want this for their sons, especially the moms who worked so hard to raise a good man.

Men and women need each other. If you're a mom who wants to reject the dominant culture, support your son, and communicate effectively, these tips will help.

USE PARTNERSHIP SKILLS, NOT PARENTING SKILLS

This one can be difficult at first. It is much easier to talk in parent mode. I have found myself slipping into it from time to time. It is so unattractive and leaves me feeling like an annoying mother and leaves my son feeling like an annoyed child.

Not good.

For empty nesting to be successful, your relationship must take on a new level of communication and deeper (yes, deeper) meaning. Communicating as adult partners—rather than parent and child—is the way to go.

Your job as the parent in charge is done. When your son is a senior in high school, spring is drawing near, and the summer and fall lie ahead, you need to pull back on the mom thing and be there for counsel and advice—and only if he asks for it.

"It's true, it's simple like that. I didn't need to be a helicopter parent or a lawnmower parent," says Laura. "I'm not the parent anymore. I really am a partner. About six months after that conversation in Starbucks, we did a Kickstarter for his wine condom idea, and my son started his entrepreneurial venture. And he's doing it. He's paying his own ride."

Partnership requires vulnerability, just like Laura experienced with her son when he told her he was lost. Instead of "sucking it up," we must "cough it up" instead. We must express what we feel and what we think and allow our sons the space to do the same.

Dr. Beth Halbert counsels lots of parents with growing teenagers or adult children and points out that their kids want to have real communication with them. "The key with this is, your kids are thinking *can you handle my truth?*" says Beth. "Can you handle as a parent my authentic self? Can you handle as a parent if I'm gay? Can you handle that I smoke pot? Can you handle if I have an interracial marriage? Can you handle if I have a child out of wedlock? Can you handle if I have big feelings about something that happened when I was three years old? Can you handle, can you handle, can you handle?"

Can you?

It is absolutely true that your child is thinking, "If you deny my reality, judge me, correct me, critique me, criticize me, fix me, or need to make me different or better in any way, then I don't want to be around you," Beth says. "Young clients say, 'It's too painful, because then I feel like I have failed, myself and you as my mom.'"

For your teenager, that can look like the silent treatment. I know I experienced that one a few times. For your adult child, that can look like I'm too busy to see you.

"So, if I, as the adulting child, am going through a whole bunch of feelings, and I think these awful feelings are going to hurt you, then I'm going to go hide in my room and play video games and not engage," says Beth. "And this is true for anyone and everyone on this planet. Spouses. Husbands. Siblings. Parents. Anybody. However, if you can handle me and love me as I am, then why in the world wouldn't I want to spend time with you?"

Don't baby him

David Villella is a performer with "Vegas! The Show." He has worked in this production for about 15 years. He owns a house, loves his partner, and takes care of his many pets. He also loves his mother, who had recently called to check on him when he had the flu. "I know she wants to nurture me because that's what a loving mom does," David says. "But I'm a grown ass man! Having my Jewish mother call me to tell me what to do when I'm sick leaves me feeling like a teenage boy who gets mad and then wants to rebel!

"I know your mother is always your mother. My mom says, 'It's my job as a mother to make sure you're ok,'" David says. "But c'mon, Ma. Can you do your job another way? That was your job when I was ten!"

Don't brandish approval or disapproval

One of the mistakes moms can make is trying to control our son's behavior by using the cudgel of approval or disapproval. It doesn't work. All it does is create distance and disconnection.

When my son and I were still living together, I always honored his personal space by leaving his room to himself. I never entered without his permission, or if I had to go in when he wasn't around, I was sure to tell him why. One day after he graduated high school, I knocked on his door. When he told me to come in, I saw a new poster on his wall. It was a picture of five naked women sitting in a row on a low wall with their backs covered in symbols and graffiti. I said, almost choking, "Cool poster. What is it?" He said, "Pink Floyd, mom." I said, "Ah," I said, turning to leave. "Their posters are a lot different than when I was a teen."

What I saw on that poster was five objectified women. What my son saw was art and beauty. My instincts wanted to take it down and say, "Not in my house! I don't approve!" But I quietly left and closed his door.

Later that day, he emerged from his room and said, "I'm surprised by your reaction to my poster, given your point of view about objectification and all."

"Hey, it's nothing I'd hang in my living room, but that's still your room, and it's above your desk. You like it, so there you go."

"That is very adult of you," he said.

Don't say I told you so and don't fix it

As a parent in partnership, you realize you have to leave room for errors and contingencies. Fred Miller, the single dad of two, says, "As long as you know their heart is in the right place, if they make a mistake, it was a mistake of the mind. I've never been that guy to say, 'I told you so.' That's just not been my character," Fred says. "I know it's said out of frustration, but that's how kids turn off from you, when you say things like, 'You should have done it this way, or you shouldn't have done that.'"

Another "part" of partnership is not looking to answer the question or to solve the problem. "If you come to me with something, I just don't try to fix it. I listen," says Fred. "Unless my child asks me a direct question, and that is, 'What would you do?' It has to be in question form. If it's just a statement, I don't respond to it. I just listen."

Listen to learn

Most people listen for whether they agree or disagree with what's being said. They prepare their reply while the person is still speaking and then wait for their chance to respond. Even worse, sometimes we just interrupt.

Women are naturals at listening to what we agree with in order to form connection with fellow women. This is what "girl talk" is all about. It gives us "feels" when we share a common idea or experience. Men, on the other hand, listen for "what is the point" or "what is the problem?"

But if you're listening to learn, you can discover a lot about your son. Listening to learn means asking yourself these questions:

- What matters to him?
- What is important to him?
- What does he care about?
- What makes him tick?

My son had been dealing with going in and out of college for a few years. He pondered where to go next, how to pay for it, what he wanted to major in, etc. He missed going one semester, even though it was his intention to go. As a mom, it's certainly not my job to force him to go back to school. I knew he planned to finish all the paperwork and loan applications and Pell grant submissions early, so he'd be ready for the next semester. One night on the phone, I asked, "So, did you get everything worked out?" That was a mistake. His answer was gruff and not really an answer.

He came over for dinner shortly after that conversation.

"Mom, I really don't like having to talk about school. It puts me in a position to have to explain," he said. "When people ask me, and I haven't done it yet, it makes me feel bad about myself. It's embarrassing. I don't want to talk about it or answer that question anymore."

"I get it," I said. "The same thing happened to me for years while I was trying to become an author. 'Hey, how's your book coming along?' And I'm like, um, oh, look down, explain my life problems."

It does suck when you're forced to look at yourself as a result of the questions of others. My son did not need my disapproval. He needed my understanding. And when he got that, he was free to express himself for the rest of the evening.

Do you see the values he was revealing? He values his reputation. He values his self-respect. As moms, we can easily support that. And a better question the next time would be, 'Is there anything I can do to support you?' or 'Is there anything you need from me to help you?'

When the pandemic happened, forcing multitudes of young people to drastically change or forego their natural and important rites of passage, Everett's college plans were derailed once again. When campus classes moved to online lectures, he simply stated, "Why would I spend thousands of dollars on something I can get on YouTube for free?"

Wait for the well

When I attended the "Making Sense of Men" workshop taught by Alison Armstrong, I learned one of the best pieces of communication advice I've ever heard. It's a fascinating fact about men.

It takes boys and men longer to answer questions. They go into their heads first and consider their answer before replying. When women are asked questions, we typically answer them right off the bat. We're used to talking with our girlfriends, and it's very give-and-take, open-ended, and very quick. We don't need much time to think. We feel, exchange, and engage. It's just conversation.

Whereas men take time to think, because they want their answers to be accurate.

Unfortunately, if women don't hear an answer immediately, we may ask the question in a different way. And then the man chases the answer to the new question. Silence again. Then we might offer options for an answer, such as, "Do you think it might be this, or do you think it might be that?" Silence again as he ponders the new question.

The next time you ask your son a question, put imaginary duct tape over your mouth and wait for his answer. Wait for the well. Let him formulate his reply. Show him the gift of patience. The answer you receive will probably be something you can learn from and support. That type of communication will build trust between you and your son even more.

Don't interrogate

It's critically important for a mom to ask value-based questions rather than logistical ones like, 'Where did you go?' and 'What did you do?' That's a mom asking for details, and it's not received well.

Picture yourself as a teenager or young adult. How did you respond when your mom or dad asked, "How was school today?" or "What's new?" I'm guessing the answers might have been "fine" and "nothing," respectively. I suspect you never gave much information to your parents, and the same is likely true of your son—unless it was something really dramatic, like a fire in the hallway or an early dismissal for snow.

One way to elicit information is to share about yourself. Instead of asking, 'How was work?' or 'How was school?' you could offer these conversation starters about you instead: "You know what happened to me today? You know what some jerk did today? You wanna hear something great that happened?"

Share of yourself freely, and you'll raise an adult who does the same.

Show appreciation

This is simple. Whatever you want more of from your son, appreciate him for providing it. Whether it's a phone call to let you know they're all right, a gesture that makes you feel loved, or an unexpected compliment, show your appreciation. Being appreciated for anything makes someone want to do it even more.

Don't shoot the messenger

One night, Everett came out of his room, very excited about something he'd found out.

"Mom, I just realized that I never really understood what an author meant until I heard the author read his book out loud on TV," he said.

"Interesting," I said. "That may mean you're more of an auditory learner. Good to know."

"Yeah. It was good to 'get' what they were trying to say in the book."

"Cool. So, what show were you watching where an author read?" I asked, anticipating some laudatory show that I must watch immediately.

"Family Guy."

LET YOUR CHILD KNOW WHAT YOU NEED FROM THEM

Letting your child know what you need from them if they leave for college is an important "part" of partnering with your child. If you are providing money, tuition, or housing expenses, you have a right to expect certain things in return. Make sure your expectations are clear before they leave the nest.

Parent's "rights"

Let's say as a parent you're paying for your child's education. You're still supporting them financially in every way. You have a right to expect that they go to school, let you know their grades, and keep you updated about what's going on in terms of school. Let them know what you need from them. You have a right to know. You are still paying their way.

I'm not talking about nagging or checking in on them. I'm not saying you should expect them to call you every Friday at 5 pm to tell you where they're going for the weekend. Nothing like that.

A friend told me a story about a father who had raised his son in a rather conservative household. By conservative I don't mean the political version of whatever conservative means; my friend was talking about respect and rules and discipline, things like that. So, this father was spending about $50,000 a year for his son to go to school. Within a year or so, he witnessed a change in his son's attitude. When his son would return from school, he was disrespectful, questioned his father's political beliefs, became anti-everything, ridiculed his mother and father's way of life, and worse.

This father still deserves every amount of respect from his son. Instead, he's actually *paying* for his son to learn about shutting down freedom of speech, disrespecting his country, discounting different opinions, supporting anti-Semitism, and other ideological things that were counter to everything his parents had taught him. He treated his father with utter disdain and made fun of his opinions and values. That father has every right to stop paying for his college. He could say, "Hey, if this is what you're doing with the money I'm spending, find your own money. Make it your own way."

Five years after writing the first edition of this book, there are now legions of parents of college students who've spent good money on sometimes worthless educations that did more to indoctrinate and churn out activists instead of educating and inspiring responsible, fruitful citizens and adults. These parents were unprepared for the personality changes and unfettered hatred their children embodied for whatever cause célèbres came next.

As your son prepares to enter college, do your due diligence beforehand about each school's values and curricula. Do what you can to inoculate him against anti-American ideology, such as Marxism and communism, and know you can set boundaries with your young adult children. If they're going through behavioral changes that are antithetical to the way you raised them, and they bring that attitude of disrespect into your home, you have every right as a parent to call it out and stop paying for it. Money talks.

Communicate rules when they come home for long periods of time

When your adult child comes home from school for the summer or simply has to return home in order to reboot, don't become a mom and a maid. It's easy to do because it's natural for you to want to be the nurturer again. But don't. All the rules that applied before they left still apply.

Let go of what was

I was at a doctor's appointment when the nurse asked me, "What do you do?" I excitedly told her about this book and wanting to help women navigate this phase of life. She candidly shared a recent story where her daughter was coming back from school for a weekend, and the mom wanted to spend some time together with her daughter, like shopping or running errands or having lunch. But her daughter was busy with other plans. Home was the only place where she'd be seeing her mom. The nurse told me, "It just kept banging me in the head that she didn't want to spend time with me. *Me!* I'll just never forget when that hit me between the eyes."

This learning how to parent adult children thing is really fun.

Parenting as a partner will save your heart by helping you to manage your expectations and enjoy all the moments you have with them. Do your "part" of the communication and let your child do the same.

CHAPTER THREE
Hormones: His and Yours

Hormones impact the dynamics between a mom and her growing son in many ways, whether mom is perimenopausal, menopausal, or not.

Many women in their late thirties or early forties have teenage sons. Their hormones can be just as messed up as a menopausal woman in her fifties, like me. My body suddenly had a will of its own that overrode any attempts I made to maintain my weight, sleep well, focus on work, be in a cheerful mood, or master my emotions. The frustration of not knowing what was happening to my body was just as bad as the symptoms themselves.

Before and during empty nesting, a mom needs all the love, support, compassion, and hormonal health she can get.

I didn't realize how bad things were for me and also, as a result, my son during his last six months of high school and about a year after that. My menstrual cycle abruptly stopped when I was almost 54. Two weeks later, the hair on both sides of my temples fell out. I would find strands of my hair everywhere in the coming months—in the refrigerator, on the walls, in the utensil drawer, in the corners of every room, and in my bed. I ruminated in despair, which exacerbated my already suffering body. A full night's sleep became a rarity. My confidence and energy plummeted.

Apparently, I also became angry. As my son's graduation date approached, I thought I was acting my same ol' self and doing pretty well at containing my emotional state that could be triggered by a sentimental moment, a meaningful conversation, or the calendar days charging toward his graduation. I also thought the arguments my son and I were suddenly having more often than in the entire 17 years prior were pretty much his fault. I chalked them up to *his* growing pains, *his* age, *his* rebellion. I looked at his behavior as something I needed to parent away.

Hindsight is a remarkable thing when it's only your eyes doing the looking. But my son has hindsight as well, and he felt no reluctance about telling me how angry I was and how difficult it was to live with me that year. *Me? Angry?*

Yes. Really bad. I have been writing what author Julia Cameron calls "morning pages" since 1997. It's a practice of writing three pages long-hand in a notebook every morning. When I pulled out the notebooks written during 2013 and 2014 for material for this book, I discovered how many times I wrote about being angry, upset, worried, or annoyed about something.

My poor kid. I had no idea. And poor me. I was suffering and had no idea how to fix it.

Shortly after I lost my hair and sought medical help from my primary care provider, my gynecologist, and even my hairstylist, I was told in one way or another, "Well, that happens with age you know." And I would reply, "I'm the same age that I was two weeks ago!"

What followed were several years of hormonal imbalance, searing hot flashes, disturbed sleep, and myriad other symptoms that were as random as they were debilitating. I was being told this was "normal." I was even told that, unless this was a "quality of life" issue, hormone replacement therapy was a last resort. So many of the health practitioners I saw during this time were in their thirties. The last one who said this to me was a young mother of a two-year-old. I wanted to ask her if Midol and tampons were a "quality of life" issue that she had to prove she needed in order to access them.

My attempts to receive bioidentical hormone relief were met with "we don't believe in that" from two different gynecologists.

All the while my hair continued to fall out, my vitality left me, and I gained 30 pounds in one four-month period. This happened even though I maintained the same eating habits and five-times-per-week exercise routine I had been doing for 20 years. I had to go outside my insurance to a wellness center and compound care pharmacy that offered more comprehensive and open-minded female care. My out-of-pocket hormone habit cost me about $500 a month in addition to the costs for tests and visits with the nurse practitioners. Even though I started to feel better, I soon could no longer afford my hormone habit. My lack of wellness became worse for years.

Many women suffer from any or all of my symptoms. Some experience urinary tract infections, depression, mood swings, painful intercourse, low libido, anxiety, brain fog, and crushing fatigue. Add to that the emotional tsunamis that come with empty nesting, and women are left wondering, "What the hell is going on?!" I know that a particular wail of mine was, "Why can't someone help me?"

If you are experiencing a lack of "yourself" and suspect hormonal imbalance may be the culprit, read on my fellow mom.

THE BASICS OF YOUR HORMONES

Progesterone

"Progesterone is the life-giving hormone," says Lori Finlay, MSN, NP, CNS, BCC, functional health coach, and author of the award-winning and best-selling book, *Create the Vitality You Crave* (edited by yours truly in 2024). "From progesterone, all other hormones are made. In the biochemical pathway, it starts with cholesterol, and then it forms pregnenolone, and then progesterone. It is the precursor to all of our hormones, including estrogen, testosterone, and cortisol, so having enough in our system is critically important." When we reach perimenopause and menopause, our progesterone levels can drop 75 percent, just like that, and our estrogen can drop about 35 percent."

Estrogen

"Estrogen is the feel-good hormone," Lori says. For healthy hormonal harmony, or *balance*, our progesterone to estrogen ratio should always be 20:1. Our dramatic drop in progesterone wreaks havoc and creates a lot of symptoms related to estrogen dominance. "With estrogen dominance comes horrific physical problems, including weight gain, problems with your hair, fibroids, osteoporosis, heart disease, breast cancer, and dysfunctional bleeding," Lori says. "Estrogen dominance is wicked to deal with, including from an emotional standpoint."

Earlier in our lives, Lori says that estrogen dominance leads to a whole other set of problems. It contributes to acne, irregular periods, infertility, and miscarriages. Traditional health care providers will put you on synthetic hormones. Synthetic hormones dramatically exacerbate the problem, which is what happened to me.

As Lori explains, they are basically fake or foreign xenoestrogens, which will tip you further down the estrogen dominant scale. "I've seen plenty of women in my practice who have sought help with vaginal dryness and were given some fake estrogen. Then, she drops further into estrogen dominance which is known to cause all kinds of health problems, from tremendous weight gain to breast cancer.

"Let me just give you a visual for a second," Lori says. "Let's say you have two one-gallon water jugs. If you start at 100%, or two full jugs—one with estrogen and one with progesterone—and you empty out 30 to 50 percent of the water from one jug, that's how much your estrogen has dropped. Now, empty the water from the progesterone jug until it is completely empty. That's estrogen dominance." Remember, it should be a 20:1 ratio for progesterone to estrogen—always. If you add xenoestrogens, then those disrupt the function of your endocrine system.

As we go through life, we are exposed to toxins in our food, environment, cleaning products, and even our personal skin care products. "Fake estrogen added to our already polluted system makes the problem worse," says Lori. "Now you have a full water jug of fake estrogen streaming through your system."

So, you're in this mess, you try and get some medical help, you are put on more synthetic hormones, and you feel the same or worse, instead of receiving answers that will support your whole body to heal. It's unfortunate that many medical professionals will test your hormone levels, see that they're 'normal,' and tell you 'it's all in your head' or 'you're just getting older.'

Testosterone

"Testosterone is the energy hormone," Lori says. "Women need testosterone, too. It fuels our libido, drive, and physical energy. During menopause, your testosterone is in the tank, too. The doctors are not addressing your low testosterone, and your son's testosterone is now skyrocketing."

Doctors rarely test for a woman's testosterone. When I tried to have my testosterone levels checked, I watched as the nurse practitioner kind of scrunched her nose and dismissed me. She went to discuss the matter with a male doctor (God bless 'em, but seriously?), and his answer was that, because I'm menopausal, I obviously need estrogen."

Loss of testosterone is another hormonal issue that puts us way out of balance with our sons. We're in severe hormonal depletion compared to them, and it impacts our behavior and relationship. Moms can end up thinking, "Where is the son who used to be easy?" And your son is thinking, "Where is the mom who used to be fun?"

Hormones are communicators

Hormones send communication signals to our cells throughout the body in order for them to function properly. "Lab tests could say your estrogen is totally fine, your progesterone is absolutely normal, and your testosterone levels either don't matter or are completely normal," Lori says. "Western medical practitioners send you out the door with synthetic progesterone and/or estrogen, while often dismissing your symptoms as age-related. Functional medicine looks at the whole body, asking *What is going wrong with the body? Why is this testosterone that's circulating through the body not getting to the cell, so it can receive the necessary communication?"*

The answer is the cell receptors aren't working properly. Your cell receptors are most likely clogged with toxins, xenoestrogens, and endocrine disrupters.

Lori uses a cell phone as a metaphor to explain what's happening. "Our cellphone could be 100% charged, meaning the hormone tank is full," she says. "But what if we've only got one bar instead of four bars for the signal? The communication won't be effective. It's the same with our bodies—communication from the hormones is not getting into the cell.

"Your biochemical pathways desperately need phytoestrogens, vitamins, minerals, and good hydration. Good hydration means drinking half of your body weight in water every day," Lori says. "If you don't detox and get rid of the junk in your body, then your receptor sites are going to be completely plugged up.

"You're not going to get the communication from your testosterone or your estrogen that goes to your vagina and says, 'Lubricate me, baby,'" Lori says. "Or goes to your brain and says, 'Calm me down,' or goes to your adrenal and says, 'Make some estrogen for me, since my ovaries are shrinking and aren't producing hormones anymore.'"

Many 50ish women are in search of "the fix" for menopause symptoms such as belly fat, fatigue, anxiety, hot flashes, poor sleep, and low libido. "They often end up in the doctor's office having a discussion about hormone replacement therapy (HRT) and then, in many cases, are also prescribed anti-depressants," explains Lana M. Kontos, a Board-Certified Naturopathic Doctor and Trained and Certified Diet and Lifestyle Intervention Practitioner. Like Lori, Lana cautions about the dark side of HRT. "There can be side effects of injecting hormones into the body, including carpal tunnel, joint pain, and water weight gain. The well-meaning doctor can hit a vessel or give you too much, and the hormones can remain in the adipose tissue instead of being metabolized. It's also expensive, ranging from $2,000 to $7,000 a month." Lana does not recommend HRT unless a woman has had a hysterectomy during her child-bearing years due to cancer or other circumstances. "This is a discussion to have with your doctor," Lana says. "And always get a second opinion!"

HORMONES AND OUR BEHAVIOR

Men depend upon our feminine energy and our female hormones. "We are their life source, especially as a mom," Lori says. "We were designed that way." As boys grow into their manhood, moms are still their life source, and they still depend upon us. Lori says, "I think they're looking to us and their relationship with their mothers as a way to teach them answers to questions like, 'How do I deal with women? How do I deal with women and hormones?' 'How do I navigate this? This is scary.'" Moms and women have to keep that in mind. "I think that it can just be really scary for a growing man, like 'Geez, I'm going to be living with a woman like this!'" Remember, women in their thirties and forties can have significant hormonal symptoms, too, including uterine fibroids, breast fibroids, birth control problems, irregular periods, heavy periods, and infertility, to name a few. It's not just menopausal women.

Then there's all the emotional stuff that comes with being cranky from disturbed sleep or full-fledged sleep deprivation. The emotional issues of depression, anxiety, and irritability can be profound in the perimenopausal and menopausal years. I definitely experienced all three—the emotional trifecta.

By all counts, according to my son, our last year of living together was like living in a madhouse. And I was the mad hatter. I wish I had known then what I know now about how much my emotions and behavior were affected by my changing body chemistry. I would have been able to address my well-being more proactively, and we could have lived that year without so much unnecessary and abnormal drama.

Lori Finlay calls this emotional trauma rendered by our hormones an abandonment or attachment wound—when a young son who is going into manhood becomes disconnected from his life source. "The more I learn about psychology and about abandonment wounds and attachment wounds, the more I can see what a vulnerable time this is for a boy when his mother disappears," she says. "They are very attached to us, and I think they need us to be attached during that time of rapid growth. Instead, they're like, 'Where did my mother go? Where did my life source go?'"

I'm sad to say this was true for my son. His mom disappeared.

When our hormones crash, and our essence is nowhere to be found, and we're trying to figure out and recover from whatever the hell is going on with us, we are cranky, miserable, depressed, and fatigued. "I think our sons become afraid of us. They step away," Lori says. "Anytime there's incredible discord, that relationship suffers a wound, especially if you're the child. One of the biggest things that's going on unconsciously is that they don't feel safe, and they feel unattached to this person who was their life source." It's an extremely vulnerable time.

I had to own and apologize for the many, many moments of being angry or detached. He was only 17 and then 18 when menopause just took me out. Being a single mom with all the accompanying stressors had already taken its toll on my well-being. My life ran on stress and adrenaline most of the time. Menopause diminished me even more than I realized.

HORMONAL HELP FOR YOU

There are many options available to you for help with your hormonal balance. Moms need to prepare themselves and start healing their bodies so that, by the time they do become perimenopausal, they're already feeling better. Moms also need to rely on women's hormonal health specialists when considering hormone replacement therapy. Bioidentical hormones are readily available now. See the Resources section at the back of this book for recommendations.

I personally recommend a homeopathic remedy in an FDA-registered gel form that has been around for 20+ years with a 93% customer retention rate. It's that good. You can find the link in the Resources section. This one of a kind, safe, microdosed HGH gel has worked wonders for me and my well-being.

Another product I am passionate about is the All-Natural Women's Hormone Kit available from Rowe Casa Organics. After using these soothing drops for about two weeks, my chiropractor saw me and said, "You are so happy. You look radiant. Whatever you're doing, don't stop."

Women are wise, and we all want to feel strong and beautiful. Since using the gel, I feel like a new person. Remember when I told you my hair fell out? Well, it continued to get thinner and thinner with each passing year. But after one year on the gel, my hair grew back, and it is soft, full, and shiny again. I don't want to sell you a product, but I do want to sell you on your personal well-being. Moms are worth it. It's time to make your health your first priority. Like they say on a plane, "Put your oxygen mask on first."

THE BASICS OF HIS HORMONES

Testosterone drives your son's growth into manhood. One of my son's favorite ways to torment me as a "mommy" was when he'd be shirtless, emerge from his bedroom, come into the kitchen, hook his fingertips over the doorsill, and stretch so I'd see his underarm hair. When I did, I held up my hand, turned my head away, and shrieked "My eyes, my eyes!" Everett liked to rub it in a little more by scratching his armpits, laughing even more.

When I was studying to be a community educator through the PAX Mastery and Leadership Program with Alison Armstrong, I found a poster that showed a muscular man holding the word TESTOSTERONE above his head. It was a perfect visual for what Alison described as the effect of testosterone on a man's body.

I am an avid fitness buff. Everett grew up watching me do everything from P90X to man pushups to core work to cardio. You name it, I did it. About six months before he graduated high school, he decided to start doing P90X, too. What took me consistent exercise for 25 years to accomplish, he accomplished in about five weeks. He gained muscle definition, massive strength, and could do way more man pushups than the 100 I trained so hard to do. This he did without cardio and only three days a week of exercise. That's the power of testosterone.

But testosterone is getting a bad rap these days.

Misogyny, the hatred of women, is real and awful and has existed throughout time. Misandry, the hatred of men, is a phenomenon that has grown in cultural acceptance and even promotion for about 10 years now. I've witnessed way too many mothers and women emasculate, humiliate, and attempt to feminize their sons or other men in some vain attempt to change who they biologically have a right to be—male and loaded with testosterone.

"To make men soft does not make them safe," says Andre Paradis of Project Equinox. "It makes them dangerous. And it's getting worse. Our culture is specifically disrespecting men as a social norm—especially white men."

Teenage boys are simply trying to find their way. "They're told everywhere that they're shit, they don't matter, and they don't belong," says Andre, a husband and the father of a son and a daughter. "Professors and teachers refuse to call on them because they are male, and they're told that they need to shut up. They drown their feelings in troublesome social media and violent video games.

"What happens is, because they're loaded with testosterone, it makes teenage boys very edgy. So, when they feel disrespected to the core, they think, *okay, really, I don't belong, and you don't want me? Fine.* And they come back and make you pay for it with violence and guns," warns Andre.

Andre notes that we've been led to believe that testosterone was a dangerous drug for men, and testosterone was to be blamed for what makes men dangerous. "The culture is feminizing men while empowering women to run men over. We went too far. We need to come back to the middle," Andre says. "When men have low testosterone, they don't step into their masculine. Their testosterone doesn't grow, and then they become the guys who are driven more by estrogen. This makes them insecure and emotionally unstable. Those are the ones who lose their temper because they don't know how to control it. They become trigger happy as far as their emotions."

Because they are men and have more muscle mass, when they lose it, it's dangerous. "It's not testosterone that is dangerous; it is the *lack* of testosterone. The chemistry has been proven. Testosterone in a male keeps him grounded and calms him down emotionally and physically," Andre says. "It enables us to stay rational and thought-based and not get emotional. Estrogen is the enemy for men. Sons of single moms need interaction with healthy men to build their masculinity."

This seems quite obvious to me. When a girl needs information about how to be a woman, she needs a woman to teach her. When a boy needs information about how to be a man, he needs a man to teach him.

Chapter Four is dedicated to understanding fathers and men and recognizing the essential role they need to play in raising healthy sons. It is my hope that this information from a male and scientific perspective helps women stop and think about what the culture is saying to our sons, dads, husbands, and brothers about their immutable characteristics.

CHAPTER FOUR
Seek Wise Counsel from Trusted Men

I knew that it was men who had the most to teach me about raising a boy to be a good man. That was common sense to me. "If boys are not around men to neutralize or balance the feminine, it's not cute. It's not casual. It's a big freaking deal," says Andre Paradis.

SONS NEED MALE INFLUENCE

"My mission is to not only raise a healthy daughter, but to raise a healthy son," says Andre. "But it's a different approach. When the culture says men are inherently toxic, dangerous, not to be trusted, pigs, rapists, and criminals, I call bullshit on it all the time. It is not the strong man that does these things. It is the weak man. The men who haven't built their characters.

"A good man will instinctively protect women," Andre continues. "When an individual man is shitty and dangerous or a rapist who steals, cheats, and lies, those are the guys who had no daddy. Those are the guys who never built their character. Those are the guys who don't even know what it's like to be a man."

I've known from the time I was a young woman that men are natural givers and protectors who want to be appreciated. It is wonderful how generous and kind a good man can be. "When a mom raises them out of their masculinity, men become feminine, and they become takers. Those are the men who are dangerous," Andre says. "When they are weak, they know they don't have the mojo to compete in the world. That is why they retreat from the playing field and become a taker."

Best-selling author Jordan B. Peterson, whose lectures draw millions of views on YouTube, also warns those who think strong men are dangerous to get themselves around a weak guy and see what happens to your life. "The weak ones are the ones who snap. The weak ones are the ones who don't protect. They are the men who are dangerous," says Andre.

"They're emotionally unstable because they don't know who they are. They lose their temper. And, because of testosterone, when they lose their temper, they become dangerous. And they do horrible things," Andre says. "So, it's not softening a man that makes him safe. Helping him step into his character and his masculine side is what makes a man safe. Those are the good guys that protect you from the bad guys. That is what we do. But right now, in the culture, saying masculinity is toxic and therefore galvanizing efforts to weaken men is what is creating dangerous men by the school loads and the truckloads."

If this continues, there will be no more men around to protect us. There will be no heroes. "To make a man soft thinking they're going to be sweet and not dangerous has the opposite effect," Andre says. "Men without masculinity are manipulative liars who cheat, take your money, and say anything. They have no character. They are the worst of the worst."

SEEK WISE COUNSEL FROM TRUSTED MEN

It is sad but true that men and women are responsible for what's happening in this culture right now. "The absent men and fathers are responsible because they're absent," says Andre. "But also, the women are responsible because they're trying to crush men, as if the whole world is going to be safe if men are crushed."

I don't want my son or your son to be crushed, regardless of the color of his skin. "If you stop producing good men because the culture makes them toxic and dangerous, who's going to protect you from the bad ones? You're actually producing bad men," says Andre. "Good men protect women. Good men protect families. Good men protect those who are weaker. Good men protect naturally. So, if you make them bad, even the good guys step back and say, 'Okay, well you're on your own. You don't want me to help you? You're on your own.' Talk about feeling unsafe. If you create a culture full of weak men, just see what happens to your safety."

WHY DO WOMEN NEED MEN'S HELP IN THIS PROCESS?

As mothers, we tend to seek advice from other mothers. We are great resources for each other. The thing is, men tend to be disregarded in this process. Women rarely ask for men's advice about boys. But it is men who know best about what's up with boys because they used to be one.

Men and dads offer different perspectives

Good men want to help and provide. They want to share their advice and experience and be of service to moms, women, and children. Women often don't give them the chance to help because we think *we have to be the independent one,* and *we have to have all the answers.* It's a sign of great strength and generosity to ask for a man's help.

I asked for men's help to write this book, and I've compiled the best tips below (and added one of my own). I hope they help you.

THE TOP 13 TIPS FROM MEN

TIP: A mom's love is not enough

Our courts usually award primary custody of children to the mother in the case of divorce because of her gender and motherly traits. "The mother is the most nurturing and loving energy, right?" says Andre. "We assume that all a kid needs is a mom's love to be all right. It's not true. What happens is, if you over mother him, if you take care of him too much, you're stunting his growth into manhood. It's not the love that makes him grow into a good man. It isn't nurturing him that's going to protect him, like you would a young girl. That will not make him safe. It's the exact opposite. A mom needs to respect him and help him to believe in himself and his capabilities. That's how he becomes a great guy, a great man."

Andre explains that what happens when a woman raises a boy, she is doing so without the benefit of having the internal masculine drives that are necessary in order to develop his masculinity. Women come from love and connection and togetherness and tenderness. Those are beautiful feminine traits. However, without intentional development of his mojo as a young male, it keeps him from being able to compete—against himself, against other boys, against other men, and against the world so he can become something.

"What happens is moms feminize boys, thinking it's a better way to make them sweet and kind," Andre says. "And women who have been scorned by a bad man will say, 'I'm going to make sure he doesn't turn out like his daddy.' You're killing the boy. You're basically castrating him from the life he's capable of having. Ouch."

TIP: Male mentors are invaluable for your son

If dad is not in the picture, then seek other men for your son to learn from. "It's so important for him to connect with mentors, coaches, uncles, or grandfathers," Andre says. "He needs to reattach to a male role model if he is completely detached from his dad. He needs that, and it would actually take care of his loss."

Andre participated in the Big Brothers of America for three years. His little brother came from a divorced family, and his mom was a welfare mom with three boys. "He had no resources, was poverty driven, and living in the projects," Andre says. "Yet his mom had the clarity of mind to know she could not raise these three boys by herself. There was a piece missing that she knew she couldn't provide for them." His mom signed up her sons for Big Brothers of America, and Andre became a big brother to one of them. Recently, the young man found Andre through Facebook and drove from Canada to California to reach him. "During his stay with my family and me, all he kept saying to me were things like, 'You do know my life would have been so different without you. You taught me all the good stuff. You taught me how to be a man. I got all the good examples for my life from you that I couldn't get at home.'" He told Andre he was sure he would have ended up in prison if it hadn't been for him.

Andre says that time spent as a big brother was simple. "I was young myself," said Andre. "We just spent time together, and we shared. He got to be seen and heard. He got to have fun and be out in the world with me." I wasn't surprised when Andre told me they went on all types of *adventures*. That's what they did together, and it was nothing big or complicated, but simply spending a little time with him every weekend. "That literally gave him the self-esteem to be able to step into a good life, instead of becoming a screw up. Because the statistics of fatherless children are terrible, as everyone knows."

Children need both masculine and feminine influence in order to grow balanced. "You're missing one parent, and they're lopsided for life," Andre says. "This is true if a boy loses his mother or a daughter loses her father. They spend the rest of their life struggling with that."

TIP: Masculinity must be taught and honored

As women, we are sensitive to the personal needs of others, so out of the goodness of our hearts we'll take that too far with a boy. I know my instinct was to make sure he was good all the time, and he felt good all the time, and he was okay all the time. "That is what over nurturing a boy looks like," Andre says. "What he actually needs is a man.

"Men and boys have characteristics that are hardwired and built into their bodies. These need to be watered in order to bloom, like a seed," says Andre. "The seeds are there, but they need to be watered and brought forth by other men. Boys have it inside of them, but it has to be developed and made important for them to step into. To be masculine is to have integrity, accountability, teamwork, protecting, and providing.

"When he feels solid, then he's the man who is capable in the world. He lands back into his body with his character, and he becomes a solid male," Andre says. "Which nobody can derail from him. That's a man."

TIP: Telling a young man to "man up" is good

A man's view of sacrifice is different than a woman's view of sacrifice. Women sacrifice their sleep, time, lives, well-being, health, and their own needs for their children or other loved ones. Sacrifice for a man is doing what you have to do regardless of how you feel about it. Step into it and do it.

"Men often say something like 'man up' which women find offensive," Andre says. "On a man it's good. Like, step into it, step up. Healthy men teach young men the appropriate use of strength, because we're stronger, bigger, louder, and pushier. You need a man to help boys calibrate that stuff in the world."

TIP: You have to follow through on threats

"When Andrew was very little, I spanked him one time because he was misbehaving. I had warned him if he didn't stop, I'd spank him," says Bruce. "And I did, because as a parent you can't really make threats unless you're prepared to carry through, even if it's something you wish you hadn't said."

It is true that, as a general rule, if you make a threat you have to carry it out. Otherwise, your word will mean nothing. "And I hated it," Bruce says. "That was kind of a turning point in a sense for me. I thought, that's not how you deal with a kid, especially a smart kid. You have to deal with them differently. Saying things like 'because I tell you to' or 'I'm bigger than you' were not the messages I wanted to send. It's a dumbass way to raise kids. Even though I was spanked as a kid, and I don't think anything of it."

Bruce remembers that his grandfather didn't spank his mom or his uncle. "He never laid a hand on either of them, and that was way back when that's what you did when raising kids," says Bruce. "I often think of him because, like I said, I don't think anything of it when parents do it. It's just that when I did it, I thought 'nah, that's not for me.'"

MY TIP: Know when to let a threat go

When Everett was sixteen, and we were flying back to Louisville from San Diego, we had a layover at the airport in Las Vegas. Seeing an opportunity to encourage self-reliance, I suggested that he go buy a bottle of water just in case something happens on our flight. I asked him a few times to reconsider, telling him I wouldn't be giving him mine, but he kept saying, "Nah, I'm a'ight."

We boarded the plane and took our respective seats—he in the window seat and me in the aisle seat, leaving the middle seat open. After years of flying together, we agreed we would sit where we wanted according to our preferences, and that was not in the middle seat for either one of us. As the final passengers settled in, a middle-aged woman took the middle seat. After a while, she realized Everett and I were "together," though apart.

She seemed to be enjoying but not yet getting the banter that passed between us.

Shortly after the plane lined up to reach the runway, the pilot announced that there would be a delay because of something wrong with some plane in front of us. After about 15 minutes of sitting on the tarmac, the 100+ degree temperature started to bake us all. Everett pulled down the window shade.

Everett said, "Hey mom, can I have some water?"

"No," I said.

"Seriously?" he said.

"Ya. I told you to get water, you had the opportunity to get water, and you refused to get water. I'm not sacrificing what's left of mine to give to you. Did you listen to what that flight attendant said? Put your oxygen mask on first."

I lifted the now one-third-full water bottle and shook it.

"This is my oxygen mask," I said.

He sorta laughed and shook his head, saying, "Whatever, mother."

Another 15 minutes went by, and he asked again for some water since the flight attendants were no help. No one on the plane was receiving anything since we were in a holding pattern for takeoff.

"I'm guessing someone wishes he had prepared for this possibility," I said. "Let me think, who was that who suggested it?" I said as I tapped my chin as if searching for the answer. "Who was it? Oh yeah, me!"

The woman between us kept turning her head from side to side like she was watching a ping-pong game as she listened to what each of us volleyed. Everett sat back in his seat and lifted the shade to look at the steamy tarmac below.

After a minute or so, he realized the sunlight from the open window shade was reaching the woman in the middle. He turned to her earnestly.

"I'm sorry," he said. "I didn't mean for the sun to hit you. I can put the shade back down."

"I'm okay," she smiled. "Thank you, though."

And then he pulled the shade down anyway.

A moment of silence happened, until my proud mom self started to burst at the seams.

"Oh my God, I am so proud of you right now I can't even stand it!" I said, handing him the bottle. "You can have every last drop."

TIP: Even bad fathers teach

Life happens, of course. Bad men exist. Everybody has their stuff. We're all broken in some ways. And sometimes we can work it out together, and sometimes we can't. It becomes the reason for separation and divorce.

"Broken men and broken women have a challenge in being able to continue pair bonding and sticking together to raise healthy children," Andre says. "The fact is, when a boy loses his father at 6, 8, 10, or whatever, he's in many ways losing his role model. His ability to learn from his dad is in being able to discern the good characteristics of his dad as well as the bad ones." Andre remembers that from his own dad. "He was great at so many things, but he was a terrible father in a lot of ways. And a terrible husband," says Andre. "But the good stuff still came across, and the bad stuff got filtered out. As in, I decided that I'm not doing that."

Your son is able to discern good behavior from the bad. I wasn't aware of this until many recent conversations with Everett. He knows who his dad is without my opinion.

"A son is able to discern behaviors they observe in their fathers," says Andre. "They can watch and think, 'Yeah, so dad's crazy here. Dad is completely stupid here. But he does this right over here.' There is so much good in learning from both sides. Your son can see the good his father brings that he can connect to and take with him," says Andre. "And the bad, he can reject from him." Those are important distinctions to learn from a father.

Of course, there are abusive men in the world that some moms have to get their children away from in order to protect them. "But he still needs to be in the picture, if at all possible," says Andre. "The moment daddy leaves the house, the boy's confidence leaves with him. And it becomes a huge struggle for them to kind of land back in their bodies and their masculinity. This can be very devastating for him. They lose their identity at some level because daddy is gone. And they don't talk about it. They go quiet."

TIP: Seek men's advice on practical matters

Everett had to find a roommate to live in our condo once we discussed my plans to manage the Stonecote Estate property. As his mom, I wanted to tell him all about finding the right roommate. But as one male mentor said, "The problem with that is, if you're going to go about finding the roommate, you're going to find the one that's best for *you*, not a roommate that might be best for *your son*."

It's true that I wanted my son to be protected and not willingly put himself in harm's way by finding a bad roommate. As the 'landlord,' I also didn't want the condo to turn into a dilapidated man cave requiring rehab on some extreme reality makeover show.

"You want your son to be accountable for finding a great roommate," said Dan Haggerty. "Your son has the opportunity to do most of the work here, and he should if he's ever going to taste accountability." Accountability is a recurring theme important to all the men I spoke with. Dan said, "Let him figure out how to find a roommate. Let him present you with ways he's going to find people. Let him do the legwork."

Other men advised that when it comes to the rules of the house and the details of the sublease, let him do the first draft. Let him determine what he wants and expects in a roommate. Then you should review it, provide feedback, and arrive at consensus.

"When I lived in my first apartment, if my parents had insisted on establishing the rules for our conduct, we would've all gone insane," Dan said. "Rather, my roommates and I created the rules together. And we enforced them together. And it was an awesome living experience. Those guys are still some of my closest friends to this day."

TIP: Give him an opportunity to take care of himself and by extension take care of you

I was advised that when the candidates came forth as roommates based on my son's recommendations, then I should interview them as any landlord should, but as a landlord, not as a mother. "Very different," Dan says. "Let your son and the roommate agree to the rules about guests, curfews, sleepovers, etc. They're not your rules anymore, ok?"

I still reserved the right to give feedback or veto a plan outright, because I am still the mother and it was my home. "But if you do it all for him, you risk finding a roommate that *you* like, not him. And you risk diminishing the opportunity for him to be an adult, to be a man, to take care of himself, and by extension take care of you." When Dan told me that, it was another eye-opener for me, and it put my mind at ease. I never would've known that if I hadn't asked a man.

TIP: Let your kids make choices in order to own things

Some dads I spoke with said they talk amongst themselves about millennials or young adult sons in general. One man spoke about a friend who was a former business professor at a university in Texas who said that most of these kids don't seem to have any drive. "They just want someone to give them a recipe on how to get from A to B, or do these nine steps and 'voila,' you're going to be a multi-millionaire," said Bruce Dane, the actuary and father of three. "Well, gee, life doesn't work that way."

Bruce's youngest son, Luke, aspired to be an actor at age 10. When Bruce took him to participate in his auditions and then his roles in these plays, he went over the contracts and the commitment that would be required of Luke to participate. "I asked him, 'Are you willing to do all this work? This is what it entails.' He said 'yeah.' And he's always kept his word," Bruce says. "It's never been a hardship because he loves it. I think it's important when you can support a kid in making their own decisions, understanding the ramifications of the decision, understanding the commitment they're making, and having them be the ones to follow it up or fail."

Bruce remembers when Andrew was having problems in grade school with his teachers, and his mom was really concerned about it. "Mostly, he was just bored," Bruce says. "So many teachers were not able to engage one of the smartest kids in their class simply because he didn't fit in their square hole. Oh, gee, ok, sorry!"

Knowing that threats were not the solution, Bruce realized it was about getting his son to make the choice, even though he didn't really have a choice. "I told him, 'You can be bored. You can hate your teacher. You can do all that, but what you can't be is disruptive to the class. You have to try to find a way to behave yourself,'" Bruce says. They went through a few rounds, and a turning point for them was when Bruce said, "I can't go to school with you every day to make sure you behave. You have to choose to behave. If you don't choose to behave, I'll tell you that you'll come home from school every day and go to your room without privileges, TV, or company. If that's how you want to spend your day, that's fine. Or you can choose to do what you need to do, and you can have all the things that you like to have."

Here comes that word again—accountability.

Bruce says that he "put it squarely in his court. I was done. I couldn't make him. He's the one that had to be accountable for the choices he made. After that, he just started doing better himself. We still had to occasionally talk to his teachers throughout his early school years, but by junior high and high school most of that had stopped." Another thing that helped Andrew was when he got into sports. "Teamwork is important. It actually made him more disciplined."

SEEK WISE COUNSEL FROM TRUSTED MEN

TIP: Let him depend on resources more than you

If your son is attending college, there are different components added to that separation. "You have one component where a kid is old enough to live with a roommate and work, then there's another one where the kid goes away to college," says Fred Miller, the single dad, rescue diver, and security specialist. "You need to introduce the kid to separation as they're growing up, so they won't have separation anxiety. I had it. I was away from home just for two weeks on a cub scout trip and got homesick." Fred says that having opportunities to practice separating from a mom are good for sons as they grow up, and that also goes for the mother. "When it comes to college, you have to be able to have them not be so dependent as they come of that age," says Fred. "Point them toward depending on the counselors and advisors in order to seek resources for their needs, rather than depending on you to do it for them."

I posted this proud mommy moment on Facebook when Everett was 19. "Everett started college on Monday and did all the necessary paperwork and payment on his own. His manager at Wendy's chose to accommodate his school schedule so E could maintain at least 20 hours a week. Last night he shared how he wants to start dressing in a new '50s retro look with 21st century updates. I love this evolving young man. He never stops surprising me."

TIP: Advise your son to be a leader, not a follower

"I've always stressed from a young age that my son be a leader and not a follower," says Fred Miller. "Keep your path on course.

And then learn from other people's mistakes instead of creating your own. That's something I've just always really preached."

TIP: Learn from your regrets and move on

Phil Rosenblatt is an attorney and the father of two adult sons. "One of them is doing really well, and another one is in a very difficult PhD program," says Phil. "I wonder whether I was too hands off, at some level, with him. I'm not really sure." Phil discusses that his son fell somewhere on the gender spectrum, and he knew it from the time his son was young. "He perceived that the people around him, like classmates and his brother's classmates, were not going to accept him right away for being different. He kind of hunkered down and tried to conform, and I let him do that," Phil says. "Now as an adult, it's kind of come back to haunt him that he kind of closeted himself for a while. I tried to expose him to worlds where people with different gender preferences were accepted, but I think there's some anger there. Sometimes I think I should have been better about it, and sometimes I think to myself that 'y'know what, it's just a complicated job, and something is always going to go amiss. There's nothing you can do about it.'"

Bruce Dane also reflects on moments where he thinks he fell short of living up to his own beliefs and, "I acted like an idiot. I wish I hadn't done those things," he says. "And you know, that's a part of life, too, right? But I wouldn't change what I think is my underlying approach or philosophy to it. I think that is what was right. Like anyone else, I sometimes fell short."

The men I spoke with all said some version of the same thing. Mistakes are a part of life. "Because as much as we love them, they're going to do the same thing. They're going to have certain standards for themselves, and they're not always going to live up to them. Life," says Bruce.

TIP: Relax and get out of the way

"There are exceptions to every rule, and some kids have special situations," says Phil, "but I think mothers tend to find special situations where they don't exist. In my experience, by the time a kid is finished with high school and in college or in pursuit of other opportunities, it is painfully obvious that you should not be living together anymore. Any tendency a mother has to try to micromanage or know what is going on all the time really has to and should go right out the window."

Put another way, when Bruce Dane's son left for college, Bruce says, "I thought, by God he's about to embark on this great adventure, and it's some of the best years of his life, and I was jealous! I wanted to go with him. To me, it was like we had done such a good job that he was ready for that, and he did really well. I missed not having him around all the time, but it is just a natural part of life."

CHAPTER FIVE

Pre-flight Preparation for You

I wish I could tell you that, if you do everything I'm about to suggest in this chapter, you're going to empty nest unscathed by all that your mind, body, and heart are about to experience. Oh, that I wish that could be true for you.

What I do know, for sure, is that empty nesting is a *phase*. And as with all phases in life, for you and your son, this too shall pass. My hope is that you will get to the other side with as much joy and ease of operation as possible.

Empty nesting is often called a "syndrome." Throughout my years as a mom, I was never prepared to think of empty nesting as some sort of mental illness, even though it sure felt like I was losing my mind at times. Empty nesting can be an opportunity for great transformation. It is a natural process you're going to go through to get to the other side, which is to set yourself and your child free.

It comes with so much emotion though. You may pick up a baby picture and start bawling after smiling. A song he sang will move you from singing to crying.

PRE-FLIGHT PREPARATION FOR YOU

A little ditty you used to dance to, like a scene out of *Mary Poppins*, may make you move your body in child-like movements, only to recognize that your child is not there to dance with you. And then come some more tears.

Note to yourself: you're going to reminisce about all the experiences you shared with your growing child. You're going to re-live them and emote about them. If you're like me, you may also experience some regrets over things you missed out on or the times you weren't paying enough attention.

More tears.

That doesn't mean you're crazy. It's a natural part of the release process. It means you're a loving-hearted mom. That shall *never* pass.

PREPARE YOURSELF

The truth is, you must prepare yourself for anything and everything during this one- to two-year period of change. Unfortunately, that means you cannot totally be prepared, because much of it will be random and happen simultaneously.

Perhaps you have a full-time job and are parenting your parents while parenting your child as a single mom. In addition to your daily "normal" of the cumulative effects of stress on your female system, your changing hormones, your diminished capacity, your lack of sleep, and the emotional waves—which I call emotional tsunamis—mean you need to buckle your seatbelt, honey. It's going to be a bumpy ride.

Start now and take the time to take care of you. Here are some ideas to feel good and restore your sense of balance and well-being.

Have all your friends and healers at the ready

Make sure you know whom to call for whatever ails you. This is important. Know which friend can help provide what you need. If I need emotional support about motherhood, I call this person. If I need logical support about life or business, I call this person. If I need to cry my eyes out, I call this person. If I need a problem solved, I call this person. If I need support that's particular to a common mindset, I call this person. If I need female health support, I call this person.

You get it. I'm blessed to have a wide range of intimate, connected friendships. Each individual has a special gift, and they are generous to share it when I need it.

"You know what happens in an emotional tsunami? It is an emergency. It's *Houston, we have a problem*," says Dr. Lana Kontos. "By that time, the red lights are flashing. In the middle of an emergency, you only have minutes to respond, if that. Helping women prepare while their child is still in high school will begin to solve the problem that this woman doesn't even know she has yet."

My friendships are my most precious resource and lifeline. Friendship is one of my top five core values, so I am grateful that I have friends from grade school to high school to my first real job after college and beyond. I think I hoard friends like some people hoard stuff. I did not have to start reconnecting with a circle of friends after being "too busy" while being a mom.

If you haven't been nurturing your friendships, do it now.

"Work on cultivating girlfriend relationships," says Dr. Lana. "This is the time to connect with girlfriends and make it a priority. As single moms and working women, we're working, we're juggling, and we're over-committing." That's another way of saying we're too busy to make time for our friends.

When your son is still in high school, seek out your like-minded and like-hearted women friends. "Connect with the women who encourage you, the women you enjoy, the women who elevate you," says Dr. Lana. "Cultivate those friendships now, whether on the phone or over a quick coffee or cocktail. My girlfriends from college and I made a pact to meet at Christmas and a few times a year for dinner. I have a regular bi-weekly master mind call for 45 minutes with an intimate group of incredible women who educate, inspire, and support me. I also have a Bible study group, and we've been together for years. That group saved me. We've gone through the depths of sorrow and the heights of joy on those calls. It's a lifeline."

Surrounding yourself with supportive and like-hearted people who want to maintain their happiness, longevity, vitality, and youthfulness is one of the best ways to prepare yourself. Women are powerful beings. Women friends just ramp up the power to the nth degree. "When you put a group of like-minded mothers together, wow," says Dr. Lana. "Talk about power, intelligence, spirit, and heart."

PREPARE YOUR HEALTH

The best way to do this is to start when you're as young as possible. If you haven't started by the time you're in your fifties, your later years are just going to be a lot harder and with more ailments and prescriptions than you want to have. The women I know want to feel great, confident, beautiful, and healthy. I don't know any mom who wants to become a burden to her adult child due to health reasons.

I remember for tens of years, the only targeted advertising I saw of people in their fifties and sixties was for prescription medications for every ailment known or unknown to humankind. There were devices galore to make life simpler, but the obvious side effect was decreased mobility—such as clappers to turn off lights; remote controls for everything; crabby looking couples in bed who snored, couldn't hear, or jostled their partners; and alert devices for women who have fallen.

I have always known and prescribed to the notion that health is wealth. I have always been determined to be responsible for my well-being. I decided long ago that I would not be one of the people in those commercials.

If you are already a fitness and health aficionado, more power to you. I hope some of these tips will enhance your practice. If you're just getting started because you know it's time, what follows is a list of the basics (some that are so familiar, and yet so often overlooked).

There are books and videos galore to explore options for improving your health and exercise routine, far too many to list here. I do recommend a few that have helped me immensely, which you'll find in the Resources section. For the most part, it's time to read good information, talk to your friends, think holistically, and take care of this one precious thing called your health.

Seek medical help from a functional health practitioner

Now that you know about your hormones, make sure you go to a functional or naturopathic health care provider. Get referrals from other women. Find a practitioner who really "gets it."

PRE-FLIGHT PREPARATION FOR YOU

"When I coach women, I use the example of a car engine," says Lori. "I don't know a lot about cars, but I at least know you need to have a clean oil pan that doesn't have a hole in it, a clean carburetor, clean filters, gas in the engine, oil in the tank, and air in the tires, right?

"You can go to the doctor, and he or she can do the normal lab tests and say, 'Oh, you're a quart low. We need to give you some hormones.' And then say, 'Oh, your estrogen's low. Let's give you a quart of estrogen,' right?" As noted, that's the problem with traditional medicine where providers just look at the lab tests instead of looking at the individual woman and what's going on functionally. It's not that they're doing anything wrong or willfully unhealthy; they simply do not have the time to perform in-depth individual analysis on everything from your mental health to your hormonal health to your daily lifestyle issues.

"The problem is, from the beginning, you had xenoestrogens and environmental toxins and cumulative stress gumming up your system. You have a dirty oil filter and a dirty carburetor and a hole in your oil pan," Lori says. "It doesn't matter if they just gave you a new quart of oil, you're still going to burn up on the freeway. You're still going to feel symptomatic and horrible."

Dr. Lana agrees. "In my practice, I share a healthier, better option. I help people look at their entire day," she says. "For example, think when Everett would come home from high school, and you worked at home. He needed food, attention, help with homework, a ride to some event, whatever it was. Well, that time of day becomes really tough for a mom now—mentally and psychologically—but she doesn't realize it." For me, I know that when he came through the front door after school and said anything from "Hi Mom" to "Yo Yo Ma," I was very happy to see him. I also knew that "my" day was over. I switched into Mommy mode for the rest of the evening until he went to bed. Then I had some short, quiet time for myself.

As I've confessed, the hours between 3 and 11 at night in our last year together were more volatile than I realized or remembered. How can you recognize your own unwanted and uncharacteristic behavior and course correct now, so you don't have to experience such turmoil or look back with regret?

"I think, sometimes, our behavior is a blind spot," says Lori. "We don't realize how cranky and crabby we're being. If we're feeling physically gross, we might correspondingly be behaving emotionally cranky and nasty to be with. We may be completely oblivious to it."

Not so our physical troubles. All we need to do is catch a glimpse in the mirror for answers to questions like, Am I gaining weight around the middle? Do I look as exhausted as I feel? Is my hair thinning? Is my skin pale? Is this what brain fog feels like? Does my appearance reveal my lack of sleep? For me, that was a yes, yes, yes, yes, yes, and a yes.

To find out if we are actually behaving differently, we may have to ask other people around us. Then be prepared to listen to what people who care about you have to say.

Don't forget, hormones impact your brain, too. "If you're noticing physical symptoms hormonally, then you may want to ask other people around you: 'I don't see my crankiness. Have you noticed that I'm crankier than usual or not as much fun to be around?'" suggests Lori.

Be prepared for the truth and then be prepared to do something about it.

Lori recalls a time when her long-time friend who is a doctor told her that it would be a lot harder for Lori to be nice without hormonal help. He asked her, "Are you going to try to manage yourself, your hormones, and your mood? Or are you going to get your body and your hormones working better so there's less to manage? You choose."

As moms and women, we want to be "nice" to our children and loved ones. But as Dr. Pete Farmer warned Lori, "People are not going to want to be around you if you're a cranky pants."

Know the questions you should be asked

When I went to see the wellness expert for the first time, I was surprised by the level of probing the nurse practitioner did. I'd never had anyone ask such deep-seated questions about what was going on with my health, my symptoms, and my life. The pharmacists and nurse practitioners at Compound Care Rx Plus in Louisville treated me like an individual woman with individual issues. By this point though, I was so miserable I just wanted someone to hand me my hormones in a jar for some instantaneous relief.

However, it's not that simple. As we know, the female body is complex.

Dr. Lana uses what she calls a three-prong trifecta when a woman comes to her for help.

"First is the completion of intake forms with a black and white medical history. The stats of her life, so to speak, including medications, supplements, and family history," Dr. Lana says. "Second, she sends me a food journal and usually blood work that focuses on more than standard blood tests. The third prong is a bullet point list about what is going on in the woman's life that I call my

'Life Bullet Form.' Most doctors don't ask for this because they simply don't have time. The medical model in the U.S. is first and foremost to do no harm." Private consultations with health practitioners give you the chance for more.

"I am like a detective with my clients," says Lana. "Everything is confidential, and I can usually dive right in, and she'll leave that phone consultation with some specific steps so that she can get the results she desires." Lana makes sure that she knows what her client's number one goal is. It could be losing 25 pounds, lowering blood pressure, stopping hot flashes, or getting a good night's sleep. "Even though I can tell from the tests that she has to address her blood pressure, my client wants to lose 25 pounds," Lana says. "So, we're going to be focused on her 25 pounds because that's what she wants. But as a trained diet and lifestyle intervention practitioner, I know the side effect will be lower blood pressure."

Detox your body

In order to support your physical health while dealing with your mental and emotional health, you need to prepare by cleansing your system. You need to start the healing process by detoxing the junk from your body and getting rid of toxic sources. Get started by drinking lots of water every day. As both Lori and Dr. Lana have recommended: drink half of your body weight in water every day.

The Environmental Working Group has a great list of the Dirty Dozen and the Clean 15. The Dirty Dozen is a list of produce and food with the most toxins. These foods are loaded with herbicides, fungicides, and yucky crap that disrupt your endocrine system. Remember, endocrine disruptors are a big part of your hormonal imbalance. Don't contribute to your troubles by eating them!

If you have budgetary concerns, but know you need to buy organic, Lori has some suggestions. "Most importantly, start with eating organic meat, because the hormones in the meat stick around forever, and trying to get rid of them is horrible," Lori says. "Then, if all you can afford after that, make it organic dairy and organic berries." Fruit that has a skin that you peel is not as critically important.

The Clean 15 gives you the best options for non-organic foods. Eat those. "You can look at the Clean 15 and go, 'Oh, I don't have to buy these organic,'" Lori says. "'I don't need organic avocados or organic lemons, that's good to know. I can save my money for my organic meats and my organic dairy.'"

Just start there. Buy organic within your budget. Avoid as many toxic foods as you can. Drink water.

When you're ready to move onto more, there are plenty of detox and cleansing programs to choose from—whether for a day, a week, or a moment. See the Resources section for more information.

Lori also recommends taking a supplement for glutathione support. Glutathione is a powerful antioxidant, detoxifier, and anti-inflammatory that helps support the function of every single cell. "I've seen women who have done everything, and their hormones are still not functioning well," Lori says. "But once they take Glutathione and work to detox and heal their body, they're just like, 'Oh, wow. I feel amazing.' Again, it's like putting oil in the tank, but forgetting that 'I've got a dirty oil filter.'"

Detox your skin

Another website provided by the Environmental Working Group is www.skindeep.org. A woman can enter any of the ingredients listed on thousands of personal care products and see if her mascara or foundation or moisturizer is on there. It most likely will be. You can find out if it's toxic, what ingredients are toxic for you, and how toxic they are.

Product labeling on skin care can be misleading. Organic skin care products might have one or two organic ingredients, but if you research the product, you can see if they're also loaded with toxins. As Lori says, "Look, having my face look good is really important, but not as important as having a healthy body."

Detox your home

The ewg.org site can also be used to check your cleaning products. Organic cleaning products are now available online and in major retail stores. "I still think one of the greatest things I discovered is Norwex cleaning products," Lori says. "They were developed by two women in Australia who wanted to reduce toxins and make our homes and bodies safer, while reducing environmental waste." The result is a microfiber with a silver in it that lasts forever, or close to it. "You can literally rub raw chicken all over your counter, take the washcloths, wipe once across your counter, and there's no more bacteria."

Exercise

You already know this, but it bears repeating. If you want to retain your mobility and your strength and your bones, then you have to get moving. Again, the younger and the sooner, the better. The fact that I've exercised for 30 years now gives me the advantage of muscle memory. That means, if there are times when my schedule or whatever interfered with my exercise habit, my muscles were conditioned to be healthy, so they rebounded more quickly when I exercised again. Now, at age 66, I still weight train and do cardio sessions five times a week, but now I only have to do 30-minute sessions that combine cardio and weight training, rather than 30 minutes of cardio and an hour of lifting weights like I used to do in my thirties and forties. My muscles are sculpted. All I have to do now is maintain them. It's so much easier.

"Exercise is so important for women, and not just for their heart," says Lori. "It helps metabolize hormones down a healthy hormone pathway. There are two estrogen metabolism pathways. It's called the 2:16 ratio. The 16 hydroxy pathway is dangerous and breast cancer causing, the 2 hydroxy pathway is healthy." Women who aren't exercising yet could take a supplement called DIM or DIM Plus. My bottle says that: Diindolylmethane support the activity of enzymes that improve estrogen metabolism. Research shows diindolylmethane increases the level of "favorable" estrogens (2-hydroxyestrogen) while reducing the level of "less favorable" estrogens (16-hydroxyestrogen).

Hydrate

You've read this about drinking water before, but if you track the amount of water you drink, you may find you're not getting as much as you thought. If you're dehydrated, your endocrine system is not going to work properly. Once I started keeping a daily food and self-care journal, I could see how much water I was missing.

My favorite tip is to drink eight ounces of warm water mixed with fresh lemon juice every morning. I follow that with a nutrient-rich green juice. Then I take my morning supplements with another eight ounces of water. If you can do simple additions like that before your morning coffee, you'll awaken your system with hydration and nourishment, and you have 16 ounces of water in your system to start your day.

Eat well for your body

There is not any one diet that fits all. "One of the reasons I do genetic testing, or genomic wellness reports, for my clients is to help them understand the diet that is specific for their genetic profile," Lori says. "That's what is going to be best for your body and reduce your risks."

Lori has experimented with her own body and the nutrition it needs, and she swears by Keto. "I felt horrible in the mornings, and I started on the ketogenic diet after six to eight weeks of studying it. It's the antithesis of what I practiced in cardiology. My adrenals had been so sick they couldn't make cortisol," Lori says. "About five months later, my doctor and I were blown away because my cortisol patterns were perfect."

I have found that eating as many organic foods as I can, eliminating as much processed food as I can (but please, sometimes I just need a microwave dinner to save time), reducing my sugar and grains, and eating real food with more fruits and vegetables works for me. I also enjoy healthy fats like cultured butter (I like Kerrygold), avocados, and healthy oils like coconut and almond oils.

SIMPLE TIPS FOR ENHANCED WELLNESS

Here's a list of some of the easiest things I did to make menopause and my changing system feel a whole lot better.

The Miracle Morning by Hal Elrod

I have been practicing this simple routine for about seven years now. This book provides easy access to the practices of meditation, visualization, affirmations, reading, exercise, and journaling. I also swear by the Insight Timer app that offers free meditations with something for everyone. When I was experiencing deep lows and breakdowns requiring transformation, Sarah Blondin was my go-to gal. Her meditations are profound.

A few pretty hand-held fans

I learned this one from the late great rock star Tina Turner, who said something like, "If we're going to be warm, we might as well carry pretty fans to cool down." I agree. Long gone are the days when I grabbed for a piece of paper or magazine or restaurant menu to give me some relief. My pretty fans went with me everywhere. I always had a few to spare as gifts when I'd see women fanning themselves with any of the aforementioned make-shift fans.

Portable greens for travel

Having a green drink once or twice a day will help your hormone metabolism. Supergreen drink mixes are available everywhere. Be sure to buy some individual packets for when you travel. That way, no matter what you eat or if you find yourself without anything healthy to eat, you can maintain your hormonal health regardless of what's on the menu.

Stand up and move away from your desk every 25 minutes

When I am working at my computer, I set a timer to ring in 25 minutes, and I get up and walk to another room to turn it off. Take a few minutes to do vinyasas, roll your shoulders back, lift your head up, bend your knees, touch your toes, take deep cleansing breaths, or do some jumping jacks. Any type of movement that gets your body off the chair and your eyes off the screen for a few minutes will do. Your body will thank you for it at the end of the day.

Exercise your eyes

It is a scientific fact that women have better peripheral vision than men. It was by design as we needed to scan the meadows during hunter/gatherer days, while men used their single focus to hunt. As we get older, stare at our computer screens, and perhaps wear glasses, women tend not to use their eye muscles as much.

Here's a quick remedy: Keep your head still. On a fixed point, look right for 15 seconds, look left for 15 seconds, up for 15, down for 15, then circle your eyes clockwise five times, and counter-clockwise five times. You'll suffer much less from eye strain and retain your gilded peripheral birthright.

PREPARE YOUR EMOTIONS

"Part of the problem with being a successful parent, and I think it happens more so for mothers than fathers, is that if you do it right, you make yourself obsolete," says Phil Rosenblatt, father of two sons and retired attorney in Boston. "So, your whole purpose for living, especially for a mom who gave up a career and stayed at home, can seem like it's gone away. At your greatest moment of success, you can feel the worst about it."

I know that was true for me.

There are tools based on science for diet, lifestyle, and mental health that will help balance emotions. Many of the tools we've discussed so far to restore and protect your health will help. The earlier you put these tools into place prior to empty nesting, the better you'll be able to handle the emotional waves, er, I mean, tsunamis you will surely experience.

"In our fifties, women usually start to think about their health and the second half of their life," says Dr. Lana. "Some may try classes like yoga, walks, Pilates, but it can still be put on the back burner because we have our child who's getting ready to graduate and go off to college or the armed services or a vocation or whatever our child dreams of. That's still our primary focus.

I really don't think we feel it or think about our emotions until we're in the throes of it."

That was also true for me. "Women operate like a fish out of water," says Dr. Lana. "We haven't been taught about this in school or at work and maybe not even by our mothers. They're feeling everything and these waves of emotions that rattle them. They're not accepted out in the world, so women just push through it and often suffer in silence."

I had long taught my son to respect a woman's or girl's emotional range, just like I would respect his right to his opinions. Emotions are a woman's GPS system, whether something doesn't feel quite right, or a movie moves you to tears, or you laugh until you cry. Women's tears reflect much more than sadness, and that can be quite confusing for a growing son.

I watched *Sleepless in Seattle* recently, and there's a crazy funny scene where the character played by Rita Wilson describes a movie scene from the original *An Affair to Remember*. As she does, her emotions take hold of her storytelling, and she ends up sobbing. The two men in the scene, Tom Hanks, who played the young son's dad, and Bill Pullman, who played Rita's husband, and the young son just look at her dumbfounded as she dissolves into weeping in about 60 seconds flat. Finally, after all three stare at her for a while with emotionless expressions, the young son says, "Are you all right?"

During many of my emotional "scenes," whether triggered by a movie or a memory, my son would come out of his room or pause our conversation and say, "Mom, do you need a hug?" Yes!

Your emotions for 18 years or so have revolved for the most part around being a good mother, making your child happy, getting them to school, making sure they're fed, and nurturing or healing any wound or injury your child suffered.

PRE-FLIGHT PREPARATION FOR YOU

Now that's all changing.

I was not prepared for my emotions. Not only that, I had no friends who were empty nesting at the same time I was, or they were married mothers with more than one child. As I've said before, when you're a single mom of an only son, it's all much more extreme. Everything takes on meaning and significance. Just like watching his first steps, you're now watching his last trip to school, his last night at home, his last time to do whatever. It's like a ticking emotional clock!

Not only that, but you may also feel enormous pressure to finish parenting. Like, to fill up all the spaces that you think aren't done yet, such as to correct a mistake you made, or to teach him a lesson you think he still needs, or to make sure he's ready. One thought which can throw any mom into a ruminating tailspin is... *was I a good mother?*

"I know when my wife, Joanne, and I took Andrew to UCLA, she was kind of distraught," says Bruce Dane. "Okay, not distraught...emotional, how about that? To me it was just normal, and I was just so happy for him." Dr. Lana has developed a similar mindset as she prepares for her own daughter who will be leaving for college in the fall. "I've thought about the day my husband and I would drop our daughter off at college for years," she said. "Parents don't start planning their child's college career when they are a junior in high school. I started when our daughter, Paras, was in third grade— the talks, the math lessons, etc.—but not in a forceful way. We presented the tools she'd need to succeed in college very early on, and she grabbed them and ran! I believe that's a big reason for my peace and deep feelings of 'no regret' now in her last year of high school. To me those feelings are priceless."

Dr. Lana has been practicing hot yoga for nearly 20 years. She says that students start the class on the floor, bended over on their knees in child's pose, which represents the beginning of life. At the end of class, students lay on their backs in meditation using shallow breaths. This is called Savasana and represents the ending of life.

"I've been in Savasana more times than I'd like to admit going over and over in my mind the very details of move-in day at college for Paras," Dr. Lana says. "Sometimes there was a tear or two at the end of class. But the more time went on, the more I talked with moms who have walked this path before me, and the more I thought about how my mom raised me and how I raised my daughter—with strength, character, and a 'glass half-full' mentality—I changed my thoughts and feelings about it all!

"Am I saying that there won't be some tears when her dad and I turn and walk out of that dorm room the first time? No. Am I saying there won't be nights when I miss hearing the garage door going up, with my daughter's car pulling in and her friends walking into the kitchen with her? No, of course not," Lana admits. "But I don't feel the end stage of Savasana anymore because this is a new stage of life—for both of us! I'm in child's pose for life with my daughter, and her college days are a part of that exciting life. She did get into her dream school, she's thrilled beyond words, and we'll be visiting and enjoying all that comes with being parents of a college student.

"I can work on more of my dreams, too. After all, we're constantly a role model for our children," Lana says. "She's going to watch how I behave on 'move-in day' and in the weeks and months to come that first year. For my part, I want it to be filled with strength, guidance, and love. I'll get an A+ in the 'Rookie

College Mom Course.' That's my promise to my new college girl! I prepared her for this next stage as her mother. I'm not perfect, but I did my job. She's ready, and she'll fly!"

PREPARE YOUR WEALTH

There are important money issues to consider now that your expenses are changing. Whether you're footing the bill for college, helping your child transition to another vocation, or figuring out how to plan for your own future expenses, it's time to take a fresh look at your finances. Eva Macias, founder of Eva Macias & Associates Financial Services and #1 best-selling author of *A Latina's Guide to Money*, advises empty nesting women to "start focusing on filling up their cup. I know a lot of the times, mothers, especially if you're a single mom, tend to want to take care of their child, want to make sure they own a home, and want to make sure they have money for college. Moms want to make sure their kids are okay, but they forget that they themselves matter, too."

Let's say you're in your fifties and have between 15 and 20 years to contribute into a retirement account. That means it's imperative to begin putting as much money in these accounts as possible. "That way, the money can take care of you, instead of taking care of your child," Eva says. "It is important that you start focusing on you. How can you take care of you?"

It's also a time to for you to factor health into your finances. Someone who's a little bit older may potentially have some health concerns come up. "So, it's extremely important you start putting as much money away in an emergency account as well as a retirement account," says Eva. "I've said this before, the fear as a woman gets older is not that you're going to pass away. The fear as you get older is *did I save enough money while my body was able to work?"*

Remember the oxygen mask metaphor. If you take care of yourself first financially, that is another way of taking caring of your child. When you take care of you, then you don't leave that responsibility to someone else, in this case your child.

"One hundred percent, yes," says Eva. "By taking care of yourself, in the long run your child will not need to take of you. I do see many clients where they're in that sandwich generation—they're taking care of their parents while still taking care of their own children. But then the cycle continues, because that child may have to take care of their kids and you at the same time. When you fill your cup, you don't put yourself or your kids in that position."

Assess your mortgage

Many single moms have a mortgage on their homes. This is a good time to assess how long it will take for you to pay off your home. And then make plans to do so. "Nothing gives a woman greater peace of mind than being secure and safe in a home that she owns," says Eva.

Assess your life insurance

Eva says, on average, single moms get 20- or 30-year policies, whether through work or their own agent. "Now is a good time to explore getting a life insurance policy that can protect you for the rest of your life," Eva says. "That means a permanent policy, so that it can take care of you until the age of 100 or 120. Why?

PRE-FLIGHT PREPARATION FOR YOU

Because technically you will be younger today than you will be tomorrow, and you will be the healthiest today than you may be in the future." With that in mind, now is the best time to prepare. "Some in their fifties may think they are too old to get a life insurance policy, but that not's true."

If you're in good health, you can still get a very competitive price. "For a 50-year-old, I would say get that permanent policy now. Imagine if you're 50, and you get yourself a 20-year or 30-year policy. But if you're 50, that means you'll only be covered until age 70 or 80. What happens if you're blessed to live longer?" Eva advises her clients to protect yourself now and get a life insurance policy that covers you until you pass. You'll thank yourself for protecting your children at the same time.

Assess your debt

Another equally important consideration is to determine how much debt you would be leaving. "If you have a home, and you're leaving a mortgage debt to someone, you may want to consider upping your life insurance," says Eva. "If you cannot afford that, make sure that you take care of what we call final expenses, meaning your kids will not have to come up with one single penny when you pass. Everything will be taken care of." I think any mom would want that.

RESTORE YOUR FEMININITY

Get out of what Alison Armstrong, author of *Making Sense of Men*, *The Queen's Code*, and many other books and online courses about understanding men, calls "manmode" or "hunter" mode. Basically, it means when you're at work and in manmode and task and deadline driven, you're functioning at a high level of productivity. You're doing your job, and you're using all the skills of a hunter. But when you come home, if you don't change back to your feminine nature of gathering, nurturing, and restoring, you'll miss out on the beauty and pleasure that comes from accessing your divine feminine self.

Return to nature and beauty

When I was managing the vendors and guests and property of the Stonecote Estate, I worked hard physically and all the time. There were very few moments for me to relax and enjoy my surroundings. On one particularly joyless evening, a downpour of rain caused the entire property to look like one giant waterfall. The water was so thick that I could not see across the driveway. I decided to run outside and dance in the rain. After a few minutes of that, I took off my top and my bra. I have never felt such solitary, sensuous, naked, and natural pleasure in my life.

Do a retreat

There is nothing more beneficial than to connect with women who are experiencing the same things as you during this time of great transition and renewal.

Giving yourself the gift of sanctuary and luxury in a beautiful and restorative setting does a soul and body good. Self-love and self-care are your two most effective tools right now. Your fellow empty nesting women seeking new adventures or ways of being can help.

PRE-FLIGHT PREPARATION FOR YOU

Take time for personal reflection

Taking the time to be still with your thoughts and emotions gives you the space to understand and manage them. One of my favorite books for personal reflection is Dawna Markova's *I Will Not Die an Unlived Life* (Conari Press, 2000). Take time to examine your past and dream about your future as you assess where you are right now as an empty nesting single mom.

CELEBRATE THAT YOU'VE GIVEN YOUR SON ROOTS AND WINGS

I forgot to do that. Creating my own obsolescence didn't feel like a victory. "It actually is, though, and I think moms are missing that part," says Bruce Dane, the actuary and father of three. "Moms go into the emotional trauma of it all, and it can override the success story. A father's perspective is different. It's wow, he turned out okay, he's entering his new life!" Bruce says this is particularly true in today's environment. "If you've got a son that's ready to fly, you should be really proud. I can't tell you how many friends who have sons in their basements living at home. I mean, it's just ridiculous."

If empty nesting goes well, in whatever shape it takes, then you've done a good job. So, feel good about that. Bruce's oldest son is now a lawyer practicing in California. "I'm extremely proud of Andrew. I will brag on him pretty easily if people give me a chance," says Bruce. "And that's part of it. I understand missing them. But it's just another aspect of your relationship. It opens the door to another phase. I kind of just think it's all good and normal."

CHAPTER SIX
Pre-flight Preparation for Your Son

A male and female cardinal raised their chicks outside my bedroom window in the little carriage house as I toiled to manage the estate. It was spectacular to be privy to one of nature's miracles unfold right before my eyes. The wonders of nature all around me is what kept me going during those early months of empty nesting.

Unlike many songbirds, both the male and female cardinals can sing. The male perched atop the highest tree and chirped in joyful trills to stake his family's claim to the territory. When the female sang from the nest, she was calling to her partner for food because the male feeds his partner as she incubates the eggs.

I watched how they taught their baby birds to leave the nest, perch on branches, wait to be fed, and eventually how to fly. Watching these parents work effectively as partners showed me many things about the differences between us and them.

Instead of demonstrating the way to use balance, talons, and wings to hop from limb to limb, we moms are getting our sons through school and homework, driving them to activities, hosting their friends, buying and cooking an ever-increasing amount of food, and eventually teaching them how to drive. Instead of teaching our baby to stay put and perch on a limb to wait for food and further instruction, we moms stay put as our baby jumps out on "limbs" like dates, work, parties, and driving as we help with their transition to adult responsibilities and all that comes with their broadening wingspan.

Birds establish boundaries for their babies, and they are ruthless. They neither immediately answer their baby's urgent pleas for food nor surrender their distance to come to immediate aid. As noted, for us moms it is our sons who do the boundary setting long before they leave home. As our sons prepare to leave the nest, single moms must prepare ourselves for the grief that comes with great loss, while birds most likely think, "done and done."

"I get how it's hard," says Bruce Dane. "But it opens a new chapter. I relate to Andrew differently now than I used to because he's an adult, and he takes care of himself basically. I'm still his dad, but it's like my work's done. If he asks me for advice I'm tickled, but I don't really expect it much anymore."

Since the time Everett was about 13, he did his own laundry, made his own breakfast, did his own homework, cleaned his own room, helped with the dishes and vacuuming, and took out the trash. He supported our family life in a way that I had delegated to him.

But supporting himself is another story. It's one thing to go to the cupboard and pour yourself a bowl of cereal and eat a banana. It's another thing to actually go to the grocery store and buy the milk, cereal, and banana. Sometimes moms don't realize the simple life lessons their sons need before they leave the nest. Here are the best tips I've discovered through experience and the help of others.

SURVIVAL LESSONS

Take them grocery shopping as a class

If you think about it, grocery stores are designed for women. Women have scan vision based on our unchanged DNA from hunter/gatherer times. We can scan rows of 20 varieties of butter and easily find the one we need. A man looks at the same rows of butter, and he has to look at each one separately to find the one he needs. He has single focus, meaning he literally looks at one thing at a time. That's why you see so many men on cell phones in grocery stores staring at the shelves and talking to their wives or partners or mothers for instructions because they're lost among the choices.

Take your son to the grocery store as a true training exercise. There are also classes available near college campuses for real-life "home economics" experiential learning. You need to show him how to look up at the signs for the aisle designations inside the store. I can't tell you how many times I would send Everett to get something, and he would come back empty-handed and say "Mom, I can't find it." I finally realized I had to say, "Honey, look up. Do you see the signs for the aisles? Do you see that aisle five has these things with these categories and subcategories?" Our young sons truly don't know this unless they're taught.

My son spent many hours of his life with me in a grocery store until he was about 15. I didn't make giving instructions about the grocery store a part of our experiences. Young men and boys tend to think of grocery stores or drug stores as one big random display of products. Just remember that he biologically sees things differently than you, and don't belittle him for it. It's easy to make a jab in a joke or a jest, but it's damaging to a growing man because he thinks there's something wrong with him. Our culture tells him that in too many ways already—don't join in the pile on.

Teach simple recipes

I realize there are probably many children who joined their moms in the kitchen and enjoyed learning to cook. My son was not one of them, just as I was not one of them with my mom. But if you teach your son to cook some simple dishes that you already know he loves, he'll eat better. Spaghetti, tuna salad, crockpot meals, and smoothies are good examples. For many months in the beginning of our empty nesting journey, when he wasn't having a meal with me, he was microwaving processed meals and buying fast food. He knew the importance of healthy eating, but he had a grab-and-go kind of lifestyle. One day he said, "Mom, I'd just like to know how to make scrambled eggs."

Remember to keep it simple. Walk them through some easy but healthy dishes that they can eat in order to supplement their fast food or college cafeteria lunches. Just make it one recipe at a time, with as few ingredients as possible.

Teach car basics

When I was his age, I was all about being Miss Independent and taught myself how to change a tire to minimize my chances of being a "damsel in distress." I taught myself how to check the oil and the window washer fluid and change the wiper blades. Everett has no interest in cars except getting in one and driving, so I had to take the time to teach him those basics.

One time when something broke down in his car and he was stranded after visiting me at the estate, he called for an on-site mobile car repair guy. I asked the man if he would allow Everett to watch and learn, and he was more than happy to offer guidance.

Teach money management skills

Financial Expert Eva Macias says that the "number one thing that I would advise a parent to teach their kids is to learn to live within their means." I remember one of the most abundant times in my life was when I lived *below* my means. I loved feeling free because of it. "Everybody can have a little bit of everything as long as they live within their budget," Eva says. "If you master your budget, you will always have money, and you will always be able to save. You'll also be able to have clothes and a social life and a car, and one day be able to own a home." Eva recommends teaching our kids to live with cash and without credit cards. "Teaching them the responsibility to live within their means will teach them to be financially successful."

Credit cards create debt and the stress that comes with it. Eva cautions that credit card overuse can be taught from parents to children and from children to parents. "Most parents tell their kids how something is supposed to be done. But kids don't normally learn from telling; they learn from seeing. They have a monkey see, monkey do mentality," Eva says. "In order for your child to live within a budget, you have to show them the way. Sit down and say, 'Look, I handle these things like this. This is what I do each month.' That is how they learn to have a relationship not only with you, but with money. As long as you can respect your money, your money will respect you right back."

Teach about saving at a younger age

As the single mom of the only nephew among my family, my son was lucky to be showered with cash and gifts. It was lucky for him as well as me, because he was able to buy the next big fashion trend and the types of things he wanted that I could not afford or simply didn't want to spend my money on.

From his grandparents and an aunt and uncle on his father's side to my three older sisters who had no children, my son was a money magnet. He loved getting money. (I wish someone had been sending me money. Instead, I had to do things like go to court to get past-due child support payments, but that's a story for another book.)

So, his having money was great. Something I would change if I could is to have taught him more about saving, giving, and budgeting when the dollars were flowing in. I strongly recommend teaching your children these things, especially when you're a single mom who may be on a strict budget. What they see you do, they'll learn.

My son had a big surprise after turning 18 and after graduating from high school. All the money stopped flowing in so freely afterward. He was no longer receiving cash from relatives "just because." It now had to be earned or waited for until birthdays and Christmas. That was a big reveal moment for him, which he didn't like and wasn't prepared for.

Manage college planning

Eva believes in the importance of a child taking responsibility for their choices and their actions, including the expenses of college. "I've seen parents who help out their kids by getting loans in their names. It is important that the child knows that the debt belongs to them," Eva says. "Even if the parent is able to pay for their child to cover two or four years of tuition, the child needs to understand that they are responsible for a portion of that debt. They get to pay back parents instead of college lenders."

Start a secret savings account

Eva offers parents some different saving and investing strategies in partnership with their children. Oftentimes, her clients who are parents would tell their children they will house them but will charge a minimal rent—nothing as expensive as an apartment or dorm expense. "Suppose that amount is $250," Eva says. "What some parents have done, instead of using that rent toward their own mortgage, is put that money aside in an account. At the end of those four years, the parent then asks their graduate, 'What is your debt now?' Let's just say they did accumulate some debt. The parent can then say, 'Here you go, you have this account that I've been holding for you, and you can now use it to pay off a portion if not all of that debt.'"

Eva thinks it's a win-win strategy. "Housing must be paid for if the child is not living at home. Instead of all that money going to someone else for rent, you're just saving it for them to live in your home. Your child is thinking, *I'm having to pay rent at home,* but he or she has no idea that for the next four years that money is going to accumulate for them.

"It's an amazing graduation present," Eva says. "You want to put it into an account that won't lose any money, which is protected against any losses in the market, and that will make money. The main goal is to give your son or daughter more than what you originally had."

It goes further than just money. It goes to teaching the child the responsibility for who they are becoming as adults. "Too many parents see their kids as *this is my son, this is my daughter, and I'm responsible* versus *I'm teaching my son or daughter responsibility*," Eva says.

Eva recalls that she had to pay about $150 to live in her parents' home. She was very upset thinking, *why should I have to pay to live in my own house?* "What I didn't know was that my parents were teaching me how to be responsible, because when I bought my home at 23, guess what? That taught me that if I could write a check for $150 every month, then I would later be able write a check for $2,000 a month for a mortgage because I knew that I had what it takes to be able to get there."

Don't insist on college

As valuable as a college degree is, it's not the only option. In fact, there are *better* options for sons who simply don't want to go to school or aren't ready. "I think that, as parents, we like the idea of college for our kids," says Terri Kendall, the school psychologist. "We think that's the best choice, but, as we know, that doesn't always happen."

College expenses are insane. If you cannot afford to pay for it, there are ways your child can get started. Community colleges are an excellent way to complete general studies for a reasonable cost. That's how I earned all my general education credits for three years or so while working full time as a receptionist and part time as a server. Only after doing that did I transfer to San Diego State University to finish my bachelor's degree. There are also different types of work studies programs, where students can work for their tuition. Pell Grants help a lot for lower income families. They helped me. In fact, by being independent at age 21 before applying for Pell Grants, I was considered poverty level and got a nice supplement for tuition in addition to the student loans I received. "Stay in touch with a financial or guidance counselor, and say, 'This is really important to our family, but financially we can't take it on,'" Terri says. "Look for ways to make it happen in a way that works for your kid and your family."

Teach him about female emotions

Remember to teach your son a simple thing like, basically speaking, women are emotion-based and men are opinion-based. Teach your son to not make fun of a girl's or woman's emotions; just as a woman shouldn't make fun of a boy's or man's opinions. Both ways of being matter and are worthy of value. Teach your kids the basics of those different experiences.

Everett treats girls and young women really well as a result of being taught to do so. As a mom, I was like his exhibit to study all things female. Instead of trying to fix a girl's emotions, ignore them completely, or feel uncomfortable around them, he asks, "Do you need a hug? Are you ok? Can I do something?"

PRE-FLIGHT PREPARATION FOR YOUR SON

Teach about birth control

Make sure you teach your son that it is his responsibility to prevent pregnancy. He needs to recognize his part of a sexual partnership. If he doesn't want an unwanted pregnancy or an unwanted abortion, it is up to him to prevent it from happening. I could not tell my son enough that he should not take it for granted that a woman is taking care of birth control, no matter what she says. Accidental pregnancies happen; sometimes they happen on purpose. Men have no say in the matter in today's culture when it comes to pregnancy and childbirth. So, if your son doesn't want to be a father, tell him he must protect himself and wear a condom. Start telling him that during adolescence. And if your son is gay, the same rule applies about condoms, just for different reasons.

One afternoon Everett and I were cleaning the garage at the condo to move more of my things into the carriage house and purge more stuff. I came across a box I wanted to use that was mostly empty, but at the bottom were innumerable empty condom wrappers.

"Alrighty then, I ain't cleaning this out. This one's yours."

He stepped over and looked down at the inside of the box and then popped his head back up.

"Oh. God. Mom. Awkward."

"Ya think?!"

What a way to find out your son is doing as he's been told.

Stop protecting them

I asked Austen Brennan, author of *Grey Wolf* and a graduate student in US Foreign Policy and National Security at the American University School of International Service, what types of things a mom should do differently. Without hesitation, he said, "A mom has got to stop trying to protect her sons from life." When I heard him say that, I realized I had protected my son longer than I should have.

I tried so hard to protect Everett's childhood— that is a worthy cause for any mom's child. I wanted to make it last as long as possible by keeping him away from video games and computers and R-rated movies and smart phones. That was extremely challenging given that the peer pressure from other parents was not on my side.

The thing is, I carried that instinct to protect too far when it came to many of the painful realities of the real world. I didn't want him to know about all the bad people and tragedies and travesties out there. I didn't want that to be a part of his life.

He found out anyway, of course, because that's how life works. But I could have done a better job of preparing him for some of the harsher realities of life. Yes, our child has to try, fail, and learn. Some lessons do have to be learned the hard way. But a little better preparation about the travails of the real world would've helped.

"I think that moms tend to want to provide kind of a rose-colored perspective on things," says Austen. "Trying to keep me, not innocent, but more protected and less exposed to the kind of underside of the world that we live in. It's not necessarily a bad thing, but it's kind of a reality that you end up having to face at some point in your life. I wish I had been prepared for it a little bit better."

Austen said that teaching him more about dealing with other people who have different motivations for things and different backgrounds and different ways of doing things would have helped. "I was interning with the sheriff's office in college, and you get exposed to a lot of people that you don't really meet growing up in a good home; people who are doing things that you don't really expect a whole lot of reasonable people to be doing."

Yolandra Drake, RN, BSN, author of *Single Parent Secrets*, and mom to a college-age daughter agrees. "You know, the only thing I probably would have worked on with her more was helping her to be more of a strong person," Yolandra says. "She was used to me being the strong one all the time. Sometimes she didn't have to step up as much as she needed to. During college she had problems dealing with people who weren't so nice. She was used to being around my friends, my family, and everyone who treated her well. Life was good. Then in college, she had confrontations with people who were just nasty. She really had a hard time dealing with that because she had been so sheltered. That's my only regret, just not preparing her more for that. I didn't really *think* to prepare her for it.

"You try to protect your kids and make life different for them, so they don't have to deal with the same issues that you had to deal with. I think it's because we're already single parents, so you're already feeling guilty about that. But life's issues and how you handle them really make you who you are. They make you stronger. But I didn't want her to have to go through it, so it definitely made me a little bit overprotective. And you can't protect them from everything, so you want to protect them from what you can!"

I can attest to that.

Austen reminds me again, though, "Just don't do everything you can to shelter them completely from the world," he says. "Because eventually they are going to have to go out into it, so it's a better idea to prepare them for what they're about to head into as opposed to keeping them in the dark."

Don't make life too comfortable

When Everett was a junior and a senior in high school, he missed the morning bus a few times. He'd come into my bedroom at 6:30 or whenever it was and wake me to drive him. I didn't have any problem at all with his not being ready to get his driver's license yet, but I did have a problem with being awakened to drive him to school because he couldn't do it himself. I'm thinking this is when some of that "cray cray" anger he told me about showed up. So, a few times, I said (or probably snarled), "Walk." Later I'd feel guilty about it, but there was no need.

"That is good parenting with a boy," says Andre Paradis of Project Equinox. "You wouldn't do this to a girl because it's unsafe. For a boy, it's completely different. You put his life back on him. He screws up, it's on him. He doesn't wake up, it's on him. He doesn't do his laundry, it's on him. It's not cruel or mean at all. It's just that he needs to be in charge of himself early on. That way it becomes a natural thing for him to handle his life.

"So, if he misses dinner time for whatever reason, whether playing basketball or whatever, and he comes home and he's hungry, that's when you need to say, 'You know where the fridge is.'

PRE-FLIGHT PREPARATION FOR YOUR SON

"If you overprotect him, over baby him, over mother him, he can't find his way," Andre continues. "The same is true if you try to control the direction of his life and choices. He becomes one of those guys who can't find his way. We have plenty of examples of these guys out there right now, living in their mom's or their parents' basement."

One extremely unfortunate example of that is the 30-year-old man who sued his parents in order to be able to remain a tenant in their home. Not only was this man a father to a young child who he was not helping to support, he worked harder to stay in his parents' basement than he would have at a job. His parents gave him a cash incentive to move out with the 30-day eviction notice they issued, but he didn't budge. The judge who heard his case threw that kid out of the house by court order.

"Right? Thirty years old and still playing video games with no job or desire to get one," Andre says. "These guys are so comfortable. The thing about males that very few women understand is a man is supposed to work. However, if he doesn't have to, he's not going to."

My son is a late bloomer, just like I was. I graduated from San Diego State University 10 years after my high school graduation, and every step I took over those years led me to the career of my dreams. I never felt pushed by my parents' or society's timetable. I felt no need to push my son beyond the steps he was ready to make; however, there's no way he'd still be living with me at age 30.

"When you make life comfortable for them, they don't leave," Andre says. "And when they don't leave, they don't do anything, and they become wet noodles in the world. They can't take care of themselves, never mind anybody else. So again, by 18 to 20, you need to let him find his way. My wife wants to go right for him, like babying him. But no, no, no. He's the one who missed the dinner time. His mom needs to take care of herself, and my son needs to take care of himself. If he doesn't do the right thing, he is the one who pays for it. The cost is always on him."

We moms need to give ourselves a break and relinquish mommy-mode. Trust him to do what needs to get done. You have to pull back from his life.

"If he's not going away to school, then you can support him for the life he's building while still at home," says Andre. "But a major goal and appropriate expectation is to get him out of the house." Not right away, not like you're kicking him to the curb, but it's the goal, nonetheless.

"I would encourage moms to keep your own emotions out of it and just be gently encouraged to move your child in one direction," says Terri Kendall, the school psychologist. "It doesn't have to be this well thought out plan. Sometimes I do have friends who have boys with learning spectrum issues, and they're struggling with trying to help them navigate job-hunting and stuff.

"Just be gently encouraging and there for guidance. A lot of *telling* works against you," Terri says. "Decisions shouldn't be based in fear. I know a lot of parents who tell their kids, 'You have to have a plan, and I want you to have this all figured out, or you're going to be failing at life.' That's all fear based. Moms and their graduating children don't have to know all the answers, but maybe just take baby steps into some direction. Sit down with your kids and say, 'Let's figure something out. If you need a little bit of a break from school, then what can you do until then? Or, if you don't quite know what you want to be, but you know you want a college education, let's check into applying for your general education courses.'"

PRE-FLIGHT PREPARATION FOR YOUR SON

Austen says that the best way for a son to prepare to go out into the world is, "Listen to your damn mother. They're always right. The more I go through life and do more things and learn about more stuff, I realize 'Oh yeah, mom was right. She told me about that.'"

He advises students not to be afraid to step outside their comfort zone. "That's something that I'm learning a little bit later, but not too late to be a bad thing," says Austen. "It's a good idea to get outside your comfort zone, use the value system your parents gave you, and apply it to your own life. Because that helps keep you anchored, and we need more people who are anchored to good morals and good values." He also advises young people to read a lot.

One thing I noticed about Everett when he entered high school, but even moreso as a senior, is that he started to take it all more seriously. And it wasn't because of anything I did. "I think by the time boys get to be juniors and seniors, it does change a little bit," says Terri. "With most of the boys I see, they usually need help with organizing, tips for how to get everything done in the time they need it done, homework advice, or how to schedule things. They ask how to focus better. They seem to be a little more conscientious about their future at that point, where they're like, 'Okay, I need to step up and figure out what I want to do next.'"

Andre's son is 18 and finishing high school. "He has his own car, and he pays his own insurance. He's planning his steps," he says. "And he's constantly asking for some version of guidance, but he's the one doing it, because he was raised that way. It's not mean or un-motherly. It's the exact opposite of that. It's building his character, and it's good for him. That is how he finds out who he is in the world. That's how he builds his self-esteem. My son is more mature than a lot of 25-year-olds I know."

Terri agrees that, in many ways, we've made life too easy for our children. "We haven't given them a reason to leave the nest. We've made life so easy," she says. "We have to give them little nudges. Loving nudges."

And just in case they have to come back home, here's some advice for that.

ROUND TWO

Even with all the best advice and planning, your child may need to return home to reboot. "To have a good relationship, the parting cannot be precipitated by something negative. The parting has to be about something positive," says Fred. "Realize that there's trial and error, and the timing has to be just right. That way, if the timing's not right, and you parted on positive terms, let them know they have a place to return, and then just do a re-do and try it again."

Especially these days, be prepared that your child might have to come home for a while. Recognize that they're coming home as adults, and don't expect them to tell you where they are going. They might just get in their car and leave without telling you because they're adults. Of course, as mentioned before, they must also contribute to the welfare of the home. When a child comes home, I know some moms go back into mommy mode, and they start cooking and cleaning and doing their laundry—like in an attempt to nurture. That's not good. That's going backward. There can be no expectation that you are going to take care of them again.

PRE-FLIGHT PREPARATION FOR YOUR SON

Phil Rosenblatt talks about his youngest son having to return home in the middle of the great recession for about 18 months. "The surprising thing was, this pain in the neck, who clearly should not have been living with us anymore from four years earlier, had turned into a really delightful young man who was a pleasure to have around," says Phil. "He wasn't so happy living with us, but we really enjoyed having him back in the house. When they come back, they're much nicer people."

After about five months of living with his roommate at the condo, Everett decided the roommate had to go. As nice, clean, and well-mannered as his first roommate was, they were not compatible. The condo was part of a community that was made up of mostly middle-aged to elderly men and women. His roommate invited young guests who often smoked pot out on the balcony throughout the day or night as Everett stayed in his room, went to work, or tried to study.

I remember how proud I was of Everett when he told me how he handled it by telling his roommate, "Look, this isn't your flophouse for partying. You need to stop it or leave." The young man left after a few weeks. Rather than immediately looking for another roommate, Everett and I huddled up in my kitchen in the carriage house about what to do next.

"I have an idea," I said. "Why don't you move in here with me and give us a chance to catch our breath and save some money while we figure out the next steps?"

CHAPTER SEVEN

Vulnerability: His and Yours

In the months leading up to his high school graduation as well as the difficult months that followed, I struggled with revealing things about myself to my son. Yes, I was more than able to cry during emotional or sentimental moments where Everett could easily make me laugh to snap me out of it or hug me 'til the tears subsided a bit. He had become my big shoulders to cry on about this mommy stuff, but the fragility and financial struggles I was enduring were kept to myself. When I think about it, I didn't really keep my troubles to myself. My troubles were internalized as rumination and negativity that became externalized as anger and difficult communication.

Revealing the negative thoughts instead of trying to suppress them or hide them would have done us both a whole lot of good. Instead, I didn't want him to worry about me. I didn't want him to know how bad things were. I mean, I hadn't figured out the solutions to anything. I was just trying to be strong in the face of remarkable challenges, and I thought it was my job to keep a stiff upper lip.

VULNERABILITY: HIS AND YOURS

THEIR VULNERABILITY

Why don't they want you to know they're vulnerable?

If your child is like most, they worry about making mistakes. They don't want to tell you about them. Dr. Beth Halbert says that most kids think, "I'm not supposed to have mistakes. If I do, that means my mom is going to make herself bad and wrong." Instead, what I hear most teenagers say is, "I don't want her to have to worry about me because I don't want mom to make my life about her life."

Dr. Halbert says that the first thing your child needs to know is that you're safe. "They want to know that you're cared for, so that they can go on and become an adult and go on and have a life without you."

Another reason your adult child doesn't want you to know if he's vulnerable and needs you is because he is trying to be an adult. He is efforting to be a man. He wants to be a knight and ride the stallion and be adventurous without having to be rescued by mom. As Everett told me once, "I don't want to feel like I'm calling my mommy." Internally, it reduces him to parent/young child, and he doesn't like feeling that way, so he doesn't want to need you.

Let your child know it's okay to need you

One of the things all parents really want to make sure our children know is that it's always safe to call, no matter what. No matter if he screws up royally or gets stuck somewhere or is drunk and unable to drive. If they've damaged something, they don't have to run away from it. Call me. Make sure they know it's okay to make mistakes. Let them know that fessing up to them is better than hiding them.

"Right after Andrew got his license, he backed into some guy when trying to park the car and his foot slipped. He left a note. The guy called Andrew, and Andrew had him call me," said Bruce. "And we paid for it after negotiating a bit about where to have it done. After it was all over, he sent me a nice note saying that I should be proud of Andrew. He said that a lot of kids would've just walked away and not left a note."

Bruce told Andrew's younger sister about it, and she laughed and said, "Who would do that? That's just dumb." But Bruce's daughter did the same thing—she left a note when she scratched a next-door neighbor's car. "The owner said, 'Don't even worry about it.' I asked if she was sure. And she said, 'It's an old car. We're done. Don't even mention it again.' They were very complimentary that Kara went over there, left a note on their door, and explained the situation. Doing the right thing and owning your stuff just pays for words. It's so much better than trying to hide it."

"One thing I tried to cultivate was an atmosphere where they could tell me anything and communicate about anything with me," says Phil. "I was afraid that they would be afraid that if they told me certain things they would get into trouble. And then they wouldn't tell me." Phil recalls that, when his oldest son was a sophomore at a progressive high school, he asked him if he'd ever been exposed to things like marijuana and alcohol. "He told me 'no,'" Phil said. "And then I told him that I knew where he went to school, and if that answer were true, then I was really worried that there was something wrong with him." He admitted to a bit, but Phil still thought he wasn't sharing the whole truth. "The important thing to me was having a relationship where he could call me at three in the morning and in trouble somewhere, and he would get the help he needed and not worry that I'd get mad at him for waking me up or being out so late."

Help them resolve their own problems without judgment

When your child knows you're a safe person to turn to, you can honor their adulthood by asking questions such as: "What do you think you should do? What do you think I should do? What do you think are the options?" By allowing them to search for answers as opposed to just offering them yourself, you honor their young adult sense of self.

Pay attention to what they're *not* asking

If you're paying attention to what your adult child is saying, you'll be able to figure out what they're *not* saying. There often are times they're trying to find out something without asking you directly. Recognize that he needs you, but he's just not going to say, "Mom, I need you! Please save me!" They're not going to say it like that. But notice when they ask it in a different way, because they really do need you.

Don't rub it in

I've seen parents who disparage their children for mistakes. When they do it in public, it's just so awful. One of my dad's favorite expressions to me after making a mistake was, *For someone who's supposed to be so smart.* Every time I made a mistake, I did my best to hide it, lie about it, or cover it up. All of that seemed better than the fear and low self-worth that came from worrying about looking "not smart."

I've seen parents complain about their kid's mistakes to other adults in front of their kids. It minimizes them. It minimizes their trust and need for you, instead of elevating your relationship to a new level of partnership.

Remember, if you disparage their mistakes, they won't call you when they make them.

YOUR VULNERABILITY

Surprises

There were many surprises that came my way as I managed the machinations of the Stonecote Estate venue over the spring and summer months. I'd accomplish an arduous task, and then *Bam,* another presented itself before the end of another day. One afternoon, after spending hours readying the venue and the property for incoming guests, I sat down in my office to try to write. Suddenly, a 15-minute thunderstorm plundered the place, inside and out. Tree branches covered the pool chairs, leaves filled the pool, the porches were flooded and the chairs overturned, and

VULNERABILITY: HIS AND YOURS

water came through the brick wall inside the kitchen and big family room. Surprises like that made me even more exhausted, harried, and vulnerable to overwhelm on top of the emotions I had already been feeling about being separate from my son.

"You think they're all grown up when you have that separation. You think there's a part where your responsibility and your connection ends with your kid," says Fred. "During that initial period of separation, I was surprised by how vulnerable I was and how emotionally torn I was as a result. It was really tough. They grew up with me, and then all of a sudden, they're not there anymore. It was one of the only times in my life that brought me to tears, outside of a person's passing who was very close to me. It was that emotional."

So, a mom isn't the only one who has emotions that catch her by surprise. "But then you realize, you never stop being a parent," Fred says. "And once that happens, you get past it."

Your best laid plans go astray

My job at the venue started well. I moved in in April when the days were sunny and the buds on every tree and in every corner of every garden burst with color and life. I loved greeting the guests who stayed at Stonecote and reveled in the beauty of the natural surroundings.

I held onto my dream of using my "spare time" to focus on building my new career as an author, even though I hadn't written a word after months. The amount of work required to launch a venue of this enormity and success took a toll on my health and well-being. The lack of payment for my services by the owners while I was paying for my son to stay in the condo caused me even greater single mom financial duress. The term "starving artist" became a reality for me, except I was working my ass off for work that should have been lauded and compensated for.

I became more and more shattered by the reality that this was not going to happen at this magnificent place. My dreams were not to be. Only the owners' were, as they reaped all the financial rewards of my efforts to make this a 5-star place.

In May, one short month after the property launched with tremendous success, I discussed with the owners that this wasn't what we thought it would be, and that I was working a 24/7 job. I reminded them that I was in charge of running a hotel, and yet the teenage girls who came into *clean* the hotel for about three or four hours after each guest were making more money than I made as the person who was *managing* the hotel. I was clear that my working their chosen 15 hours a week to pay the "rent" to allow me to live in the carriage house did not suffice, and I'd need to be paid for the 24-hour a day job that it was. Their idea was to pay me $12 an hour for any time over the 15 hours they thought the job required. That meant in the minimalist terms at least 25 hours x $12 each week (or $300 per week), though my days were always longer, and when guests were there I was never off-duty. My loss of any sense of personal time, boundaries, or safety became my norm.

One night in June, my cat had just been transferred from my son and the condo to me, and we were sitting in my little living room as she tried to make herself at home. A big and boisterous group of people were staying at the main house, and my job was to be the source of safety, emergency repairs, help with anything, and possible patrol while letting the guests alone to have a good time, as always. Suddenly, my front door was kicked open and a man carrying a beer case under each arm stepped inside my home. My cat ran from the house and out to the dark woods in fear.

"What are you doing here?!" I exclaimed.

"Oh, I thought this was the pool house," he said, and then left without apology or closing the door. As he went off to join the fun, I went out to the woods in search of my little cat. The next-door neighbor saw me looking with my flashlight in the trees on his property, and he wanted to help. He said he'd keep an eye out for her. But I never saw her again. At times I was inconsolable, but Everett reassured me that I shouldn't beat up on myself about it.

Another evening late that summer, I was in the main house, exhausted from the heat and the never-ending obligations. I was checking on things and trying to make sense of my situation with a lot more space and creature comforts than the carriage house offered. The owners and their family were off to the Virgin Islands for two weeks, leaving me without hesitation to take care of all things necessary to keep the place running. They didn't even have to bother answering emails while they were away.

I sat at the kitchen table at my computer, sitting braless and in boxer shorts. I thought I was all alone for the first time in weeks and could finally rest with my thoughts. But there was a knock at the front door.

I had no way to cover myself. I certainly couldn't ignore the knock. So, I opened the door a crack and peeked around it. There was a couple who smiled and said, "Hi, are you Lauren? We're here for our tour of the property."

Shit.

I could've turned them away. I could've said not now. I could've apologized profusely for forgetting this scheduled meeting and made them come back. Instead, I surrendered to my vulnerability and exhaustion and said I completely forgot. I told them what I was wearing, but if they didn't care, neither did I at this point.

"We don't care," they said, and came on in.

I kept my arms crossed over my chest as I gave them a tour of the inside. I really did love this part of the job, connecting with people and feeling honored to be a small part of making their special plans a reality. This fun and lovely middle-aged couple were getting married in the spring. After our meeting, they booked the property that night and even invited me to their wedding.

These types of random interruptions had become commonplace. I had become "needs central" for the home, the owners, the guests, and the vendors. I made several more attempts over the summer to schedule time with the owners to discuss these things, but the owners avoided meetings with me, or they'd schedule a time with me on a Saturday afternoon at one, but then fail to show up until four. They'd stay for no more than 15 minutes and then questioned me about what was wrong with me that I had waited for them.

One of the bright spots of my tenure was the cheerful and reliable help of the men who were the different contractors. There was the Terminix man named Antoine, who helped me so often with every pest that needed to go. There was Denny, the plumber, who fixed never-ending malfunctions with the kitchen sink over the course of the year. There was Ron, the pool guy, who came to open and shut the gorgeous salted pool for the sea-

VULNERABILITY: HIS AND YOURS

son, as well as teach me how to keep it functioning properly over the summer. There was also the neighbor Ralph, who popped in view from time to time as I mowed the five acres to fill me in on things I didn't know about the property, and who said I could call him if I ever needed help. And there was Jose, the gardener, who appeared on the property once a week to do the weeding and seeding and trimming of the many flowers and trees, after having been dropped off in the morning by his employer and left out there for the remainder of the day. (All names have been changed.)

On a particularly hot day in the middle of August, with temperatures nearing 100 and the humidity the same, I saw Jose out by one of the flower beds and brought him out a few bottles of cold water. He was quite appreciative, and we had our weekly little friendly chit chat about things that I cannot remember.

What I do remember is texting the owners to see if I could take $20 from petty cash to tip Jose. I told them the work he was doing was grueling in the heat of that day. I was shocked when the owner texted back, "No, absolutely not. I'm sure he's paid very well already."

I didn't know if it was selfishness, greed, good business, or what the owner's husband said to me one night when he was trying and failing to fix the broken pool pump on his own, which was "I know we're cheapskates."

I did know it wasn't anything I ever wanted to do or be. I wanted to give Jose $20 out of my own pocket. Given that I had worked four months by now without being paid myself, the thought was futile.

After sharing my story with a very wise friend named Kristy, she asked me simply, "What are you pretending not to know?"

They tell you things you need to hear

My son knew that I wanted to create an author life at the venue. He knew that I considered this to be my one last chance to do everything I had always talked about wanting to do. I didn't want my son to know how big this mistake had become.

Moms are known to have perfect mom syndrome that is an even fiercer version of perfect woman syndrome. It's our ideal for who we expect ourselves to be, and when it comes to being a mom, often we feel that anything less than perfect just won't do. We're either afraid to recognize that we've made a mistake, or if we do recognize it, we can be afraid to admit it because that means our kid will know we're not perfect. I didn't want my son to know my dream was falling apart. He wanted it for me as much as I did.

The thing is, your child already knows you're not perfect. I've been given two gifts by two separate men. One of the most freeing things a man ever told me was, "You do realize I know you're not perfect, right?" The other gift was from my son, when he said, "Mom, you know that moment when you realize your parents aren't perfect?"

"Yes," I said.

"Well, that moment happened a long time ago. The jig is up."

Be vulnerable enough to explain

By October, after not having earned any income and with my son returning to live with me, I was a broke and busted mess. My menopausal symptoms were only eclipsed by my growing financial despair. The owners finally met with me to discuss paying me at the end of September. They told me what a spectacular job I was doing, and they wanted me to keep doing it. They knew they would have to pay me for the past seven months' efforts, but I did not hear from them until three weeks after our meeting. The guests still came, I still provided exceptional service, and the 5-star reviews on the website kept growing, with my name mentioned on all of them.

On one particularly bad evening, after working all day, I received my cell phone bill. We had run over the data minutes, resulting in about thirty bucks of overage charges. I opened the bill in the kitchen as Everett sat at his desk nearby that we had closely positioned in the little alcove space at the top of the stairs.

My inability to pay the extra charges on that bill was my bottom. My life had become desperate and absurd. I was thinking (and saying out loud), quite upset, "Oh my God, I am 56 years old. Why am I at a stage in my life where I'm having to be upset and worried about freakin' data minutes?! A stupid freakin' thing like data minutes?!"

I angrily pulled on my shoes and yanked at the shoestrings to tie them. I had to go greet some guests who were coming to the property.

The extra data charges were because of Everett's being 19 and streaming videos on his cell phone. It shouldn't have mattered, and it only mattered because of money. I was coming down hard on myself and freaking out, *again*. I couldn't believe I had reached this point.

Even though I was speaking out loud about the data minutes, I was talking about myself. I felt like a loser and betrayed by the owners. But because I was saying this out loud, Everett took it personally. He finally stood up from his desk and yelled, "My God, mom, you're being so irrational!" He stormed down the stairs and out to the garage to start purging or sorting his belongings. We both knew it was time for us to get out of this place and had been discussing plans, and his stuff had landed everywhere in that garage after moving them from the condo.

I immediately realized that there was a complete disconnect about what my venting was about. It was about my own feelings of fear, failure, and hurt, not data minutes. But all he saw was an irrational woman who was having a meltdown over a cell phone bill!

I went out to the garage. He was mad. He used that word again, irrational. So, now I'm getting mad. Something rose up in me. I knew I had to be understood. And I certainly didn't want my son thinking my reaction was about him.

"Honey, please. Wait a minute," I said. He didn't look at me but instead kept pulling stuff out of boxes and shoving them into a black trash bag.

"What?!" he said.

"I want to show you that my reaction is normal and rational because of what I'm going through. It's not about the cell phone."

I slowed down. I took a few breaths.

"Would you please stop a second and listen?"

He stopped purging and looked at me. He crossed his arms. His expression was hardened.

"I'm not angry at you. You haven't done anything wrong. You should be able to use all the data you want without having to worry about stupid crap like this!

"I'm 56. I earned six figures at my last job. I supported us for 15 years. I should be in a place where data minutes don't matter.

VULNERABILITY: HIS AND YOURS

I've worked my ass off for the last seven months for someone else's success. We're standing outside in front of this estate that now has 15 five-star reviews, six-figure success for the owners, and destitution for me as I tried to support you in the condo and me here. Just last week, the owners paid me a lousy two-thousand-dollar check that I had to drive 15 miles to go pick up because they taped it to their back door. And here I am, after all that work, worrying about paying for a cell phone bill. This isn't about the data minutes."

"They taped it the door? They didn't even hand it to you or say thank you or anything?" he said.

"Nope," I said. "Can you see how this was a rational reaction to what I'm going through?"

I felt so vulnerable in finally saying these words out loud to him.

After thinking for a moment, he said, "Oh. Yeahhhh." His words were such a relief. He could see that his mom was not an emotionally deranged woman, but instead a worried, hurt, and devalued one.

I remembered something that Alison Armstrong had taught me. Men trust facts not feelings. Facts are a trusted source; feelings are perceived as bad facts. I needed to be responsible for the effect my feelings were having on my son. It was another chance to partner in understanding each other and move on from there. The facts of the matter were understandable.

He wasn't mad at me anymore. Instead, he gave me a hug and said, "God, mom. I'm so sorry this has happened to you."

CHAPTER EIGHT

Create "Completion" with Your Child

Completion is such an interesting topic. Not only is it a chance to purge what no longer serves you, it's a chance to say the unsaid things, answer the unanswered questions, ask what you need to know, come to terms with your family history, and move on to the next phase of your life.

When I moved out of the condo, my son and I were not "complete." There were many hardships and wounds for both of us that happened during our last year together that had not been addressed. After eight months of empty nesting, I had become even more tired and downtrodden by the life I was living. I felt devalued and deluded by the owners of the estate. Everett had struggled to find his own way during those months as well.

Everett and I really hadn't stood much of a chance to re-establish our relationship during that time of rapid change and instability. Making it an intention and taking the time to complete the past and your son's childhood can set you up for success in creating a new future as equals and partners.

CREATE "COMPLETION" WITH YOUR CHILD

DOWNSIZING

Of course, the very fact of empty nesting means there's accumulated stuff to sort, shred, or store. Your stuff, their stuff, or sentimental stuff they made as children has to be dealt with.

Laura Bartlett, the mom of two sons, said that what surprised her about downsizing was "how much crap in the house wasn't mine. Like, the bodies aren't here but all their stuff is." When Everett moved into the carriage house with me to recover and reboot, the rest of his stuff came with him. Our stuff now filled all three garage bays under the carriage house. Like Laura, I wondered *where did all this stuff come from?*

"I wasn't really aware of all the stuff," says Laura. "I transitioned into my next phase of life pretty quickly once both boys were gone. I sold my home and had to deal with unloading an entire house by myself. Now, I live in an apartment."

Here are some tips for making downsizing a whole lot easier.

Their stuff

Most moms go through the process of downsizing after their adult children leave, whether they're moving to a smaller place or creating a "she shed" in their kid's old bedroom. One of the funniest commercials I've seen is one where a middle-aged couple has totally redesigned their kitchen while their son is away at college. When he comes home, he's surprised to find his bedroom is half the size it used to be in order to make space for the kitchen to be larger. His room was now the size of a twin bed, and his parents are just so tickled to show him their newly tricked-out kitchen.

One thing our kids like us to do is store their belongings. Given that I had decided to move away from the venue, Everett had to move too, and his stuff had to go with him.

Rather than take all the decision-making upon yourself, be sure to ask your kids to participate. Ask them if something's important to them. Ask them about the things they want to keep. This also means asking their permission to throw something away.

The stuff they made

The hardest things for me to let go of as a mom were all the childhood things he created that I had been moving from home to home over nearly two decades. Y'know, the adorable and goofy things, the hand-made cards, and the many school projects. I admit I had some emotionality around finding the things he had made for me as a young boy. I mean, who wouldn't want a painted wood turkey with a clothespin attached to hold a note? They were hard to part with. I also didn't know if he wanted to keep them for his own sentimental reasons.

Rather than my having to make the decision and place the "value" on these items, I asked Everett.

"Honey," I said. "I have all these things you made, and they mean a lot to me, but I can't keep carting them around for the rest of my life. But I can't decide what to keep. Can you help me decide? What things are important to you to keep?"

One great piece of advice I received from a fellow empty nester was to take a picture of the sentimental things you've been keeping but truly don't belong in your life anymore. I wanted Everett to know that just because I was throwing something away, it didn't mean it meant nothing to me.

The result of this exercise was both practical and funny. We found one artsy-crafty thing he made when he was about seven years old. I held it up.

"What about this?" I said.

"Mom," he shook his head. "Seriously?"

"Alrighty then!" I said and tossed it in the big garbage bag.

You get the best of both worlds when downsizing this way. You get their buy-in, and the items get gone.

One down, tens of dozens more to go.

SPEAK THE TRUTH

If you're a single mom, the time may come when your son has questions about things you'd rather not discuss. As mentioned in Chapter Six, I tried to protect my son from a lot of things, but I could no longer do so. I had to tell him the truth when he asked me questions and let my son judge the information for himself.

Things they want to know about their dad

Most single moms have to face this issue. There are some moms who berate the father because the mom has her own issues, anger, and resentments, and she wants to make sure the child knows about all of them.

I felt no need to do that, but perhaps my desire to protect my son from bad information about his dad went too far on the other extreme. Everett and I left California in 2008—partly due to the financial crisis, partly because I needed a change, and partly because his father was still injecting himself in my life and causing both of us harm. There is no need for further explanation here, except to note that my intention was to protect myself and my son from further unhappiness. I had no desire to tell Everett the bad stuff, but I no longer wanted to live it either.

After a few years of living in Louisville, I finally went to court to take care of the divorce paperwork, cut the cord, receive child support, and split our remaining marital asset, the 401(k). I spent a lot of time and money on classes to learn about investing appropriately in the uncertain economy we were living in. With my share of the account, I was going to manage the money wisely, prepare for Everett's college, and then be able to confidently buy a car so Everett could have mine. I felt so enthused about being legally free and ready to be in charge of Everett's and my financial future.

Everett's dad had other plans and stole the money instead. He moved the money out of the 401(k) and into his personal checking account. He chose to give my share to the federal and state governments in early withdrawal taxes and penalties rather than provide an equal, easy, and lawful split.

It was the most avoidable and devastating financial blow a single mom can experience, I think. The utter selfishness was staggering. He wiped out his son and me, and he also wiped out his own retirement.

Everett knew of my plans to get a new car that year. Several months later, we had parked my ten-year-old Subaru and were carrying up groceries to the condo.

"Mom, whatever happened to your getting a new car?"

I swallowed hard. I wanted to cry. The truth was wretched, but lying in order to protect his father's image would have been worse.

"I've got to tell you the truth about something," I said. "I've been trying to avoid having to tell you."

CREATE "COMPLETION" WITH YOUR CHILD

"Just tell me," he said.

"Your dad stole our 401k money and hasn't paid his share of your child support for a long time. That was the money I was going to use to invest and help with your college and feel comfortable about buying a car so you could have mine knowing there was plenty of savings in the bank. But it's all gone. He could be put in jail for it. Instead, now I have to spend time and more money on another lawyer to try to get our money back."

This was not to be the last time Everett would ask me questions about his father.

Many times since my son and I empty nested, he's had random bursts of questions where he wanted to unravel mysteries about his father. After all the years of struggle that went with being a single mom, my guard was finally down. There was no one I needed to protect anymore. I didn't attack his father. There was no need.

But he wanted more details. A few years after the financial wreckage, it was safe for me to share. I was no longer carrying the emotional despair and anger related to the damage his father had caused. I could now answer Everett's questions from more of a third-party perspective, as opposed to being mired in the upset.

His questions were a big deal. They were part of his transition to adulthood. I answered with facts, honesty, and no anger. This was Everett's opportunity to come to terms with his relationship with his father.

He had questions about everyone and everything. "Dad said this thing about this" and "Dad said this once about you" and "Dad said this, is that really what that means?" With my answers he could form his own opinions. And he did.

"Oh my God, this is all making sense now!" he said.

By answering his questions honestly, Everett was able to put all the pieces of a puzzle together that he had been trying to make sense of for years. Many times, he just laughed at the numerous absurdities. For me, the important thing for Everett to know was that *nothing* was his fault or about him; there was nothing he could've done to change anything.

He gained new power with the knowledge that he didn't have to take these things personally and he certainly didn't deserve to be treated badly. That evening after dinner, he left in higher spirits because he had facts. He was not diminished by them. Remember, men trust facts, not feelings.

I may have taken too long to reveal things out of my desire to protect Everett, or maybe it was exactly the right time after all. It turned out well. I'm complete with it. So is he. I hope you can find the completion for what you need, too.

MAKE AMENDS

There are things I've done or not done that I regret. That goes with the territory of being a mom. What should also go with the territory is self-love, self-compassion, and a willingness to make things right.

"As a parent, you're just going to screw it up," Andre Paradis says. "You can't be perfect all the time. You can't say the right thing all the time. We can be reactive instead of responsive. We're humans. The only way to repair the screw ups for your kids and the way they see and respect you is for you to respect them enough to apologize."

You can say to your son or daughter, "You know what? I just had some new insight," or "I just read something that made me realize something. You remember that time I did or said (fill in the blank)? I realize now it was a bad decision, and I owe you an apology for it. I'm so sorry. I thought at the time that it was the right thing to do."

Andre says that he's had to do that with his daughter. "She pushes my buttons, so I always have to apologize for being reactive to her and losing my temper," he says. "And every time I bring something up, it could be a day or a week later, she knows exactly what I'm talking about. Her face falls for a second as she feels what she felt at the time. I apologize to her. I usually cry because I'm one of those guys. I feel bad that I hurt her or lost my temper when looking back on it.

"She'll always take it in a second, then say, 'Thank you, that's okay.' And we make amends. I tell her that I'll try not to do that again and daddy's very sorry. And can you give me a kiss if we are good?' We're good."

It is a fact that males don't have access to the data memory of details like a female does. "But the big ones are in there," Andre says. "When you want to make amends, take the big ones or the big one that you think he's stuck on. The one where he might have lost respect for you in a sense, or that was so unfair. He won't need an avalanche of the details. That won't work. He'll go blank on them.

"But, to go to him and say, 'Looking back, I'm really sorry about this. I wish I knew then what I know now. But I just need you to know that I'm sorry for (fill in the blank).' And mom, you're going to patch up his heart."

Lori Finlay agrees, while also coming at it from a different angle. "I just think saying to your child, 'I'm so sorry, I'm just learning and understanding what the impact of my menopausal years may have had on you,' she says. 'I am so sorry if you felt unsafe about my reactions. I'm so sorry if you felt that I abandoned you. I'm so sorry that I was unpredictable. I'm so sorry that my hormones and my mood impacted you, when you may have needed me the most.' You can even say things like, 'I think I failed to help you navigate these unfamiliar waters and to learn how to live with a woman and hormones, and here I was, a crazy woman with hormones!'"

Lori recommends just being straight with your kid, because even if you were there physically, you may have not been there emotionally. I know that was true for me.

Everett kept quiet about my anger at the time (except to get angry himself), because he feared that if he said something, he'd just get yelled at some more. I hope this will help any mom who reads this to know, "*I can heal this. I can fix this, so we can have a better relationship going forward.*"

FIND AN ALLEGORY

The movie *Boyhood* was released the summer when I was working at the venue. It was a phenomenal accomplishment in moviemaking, as it transpired over 12 years in real time with the same actors. The premise was simple: follow a boy from Texas, who is a child of divorce, as he grows from age six to eighteen—from kid stuff to the brink of college and adulthood. The timing matched the exact years of Everett's age from 2001 to 2013.

We both were excited about seeing the movie. Everett said he wanted to see it alone. He called me as soon as he saw it and said, "It was so unreal and surreal. It was like watching my life on the screen!" His passion was moving. "And mom, guess what song it opened with?"

CREATE "COMPLETION" WITH YOUR CHILD

"Let me think...'Yellow' by Coldplay?"

"How did you know that?"

"Well, when you were six, I'm thinking the very first song you would really remember was that one," I said. "Kind of like when I was six and hearing the Beatles. Their songs are etched in my brain."

The song was significant for both of us. I loved it, and his dad made a music video of Everett singing it to me that year for Mother's Day.

"That would be a song of high impact for you," I said.

"Ok mom, you gotta go see it so we can discuss."

"Is this a movie where I'm going to see all the mistakes I made as a mother play out before my eyes on the silver screen?"

"If that's how you choose to look at it," he said.

That was one of those mommy moments where you think, *Oh my God, how did he get so wise?*

I saw *Boyhood* the next day. Of course, it brought up all sorts of emotions and memories about his childhood, early teens, and high school graduation. As I watched, I could match it year by year to his life. He was right. It was surreal. I called him around midnight to tell him, and he said, "Ok, I'm coming over immediately."

And he did.

We had a deeply moving conversation for a few hours that night. He wanted to go over nearly every single scene in the movie, like, "Did you see how this happened? Did you see when that happened? What do you think when this happened?"

Boyhood provided an insight into our life story that we could use to discuss and compare to the life he and I lived. Thankfully, Everett could tell me all the things I did better than what happened in the movie.

I could see some of the mistakes I made that he didn't hold against me, like choosing the wrong men. It was another time for me to be vulnerable and address the scenes that were riveting to *me*, such as the way the mom did this, but I did that.

There is one scene in the movie where the son is packing up his belongings before leaving for college. He brings down one last box to put in his truck before driving away. He was really happy! But the mom was distraught. She was having an all too familiar meltdown.

Ethan, the son, says, "Mom. What's wrong? You knew I was going to leave early today."

She said, "Yeah, but I didn't expect you to be so happy about it!"

We laughed.

It was a perfect night. We tied up his childhood and that part of our life in a perfect bow. Once again, he left happier than when he came. And we could move on to the next stage.

My hope is that any mom and son can have a shared vehicle like a movie, a song, or a book to go over the things in childhood that need to be addressed, discussed, understood, and accepted so you can tie up your own bow. Everett's childhood is done and complete. That night our relationship took on a new level of connection.

CHAPTER NINE

Ten Signs You're a Good Mom

My sister, Roberta, worked as a Child Life Specialist in the burn unit at Arkansas Children's Hospital. Her opinions on all things childcare mattered to me, even though she was not a mother herself.

She loved Everett. Her little apartment was like a shrine to him. His pictures were everywhere from every year and from every age. The year before she died from ovarian cancer, she sent me a necklace with a round silver pendant that had the word "mother" engraved in 10 different languages. It is one of my all-time favorite gifts. Her best gift to me was any time she'd say, "You're such a good mother." I'll bet you're a good mother, too.

I've had a long time to ponder what I felt to be my own accomplishments as a mother. Here is my list of the top 10 signs that validate me as a mom. This list is my own and based on what's important to *me*. Yours will be different based on what's important to *you*. It's worth taking the time to recognize what you instilled in your child and acknowledge yourself as a mom.

1. **He calls to say hi**

    One of my happiest moments as a mom happened when Everett called me when he was about 20. When he calls, I usually expect that there is something to fix, attend to, sign, or pay for—

normal stuff at his age. But this time when I answered, he said, "I just called to say hi."

2. **Adults compliment his manners**

From the time my son was a young boy, he knew how important manners were. My slogan for him to remember was and remains, "Politeness is power." Yes, politeness is good and right for its own sake. Politeness also begets kudos and feel-good connection with others. It's the best way to ask for help, give appreciation, and get out of trouble. Politeness is the simplest form of kindness.

3. **He offers support for your emotions**

I am what is referred to as an empath. It's not only in my *Gene Keys* as my life's purpose, but empathy is my number one out of four top traits on my "Clifton Strengths" personality assessment. I wish this trait on no one. Besides having a woman's ordinary emotional capacity to shed tears for happy moments, sad moments, touching moments, proud moments, first moments, and empathetic moments, my heart tends to break at the suffering of innocents. I have to look away when those commercials advertise the plight of abused and abandoned animals. I've rescued everything from birds to bunnies to cats to a Great Dane who had been abandoned in the middle of nowhere. A good friend had said many times over the years about a potential movie choice, "No, you really can't go see that one. Not a good choice for you." My mom would say the same as I grew up, "No, that's not a good movie for you." My son knows that just the mention of the movie *Trainspotting* causes me to picture the dead baby scene and experience anguish. Often, he'd run out from his room to make sure I was all right when I'd be watching something like

Saving Private Ryan when the mom watches the military vehicles pull into her driveway to deliver a telegram, and she crumbles to her knees on the front porch. Tears are welling in my eyes right now as I write about that scene.

My son runs toward my tears, not away from them. By now he can recognize the difference between all those tears and either offers, "So, you're good?" or "Mom, it's okay," or "Mom, do you need a hug?" or "Mom, seriously?! You've seen that five times!"

4. **He becomes your protector**

Alison Armstrong taught that when a father or a husband or a partner says, "Be careful" or "Drive safely," what he's really saying is "I love you, and I want you to come back." Unfortunately, oftentimes when men say this to women, we can take it the wrong way. It sounds like an insult about our capability, requiring a response like, "I'm just going to the freakin' CVS. I think I can handle it." I may have been one of those women at some point in my life.

As a mom, I think I often said, "Drive safely" to Everett. I'll never forget the first time he said it to me. I was about to leave on a short road trip and wouldn't see him for a few days.

He said, "Drive safely, mom." He said it like it really meant something, not as a casual aside. Everett had moved into protector mode. Notice that transition when it happens to your son. It's a big deal.

5. **His peers like him**

The first entry-level job that Everett liked was as a delivery person for Panera. The store's location was in a hip part of urban Louisville, and it was the location closest to me. But while he worked there, he forbade me from patronizing it. I would have to get my Panera elsewhere.

A few months after he stopped working there, I was free to stop there for food. While the male cashier rang me up, I asked him casually if he'd known my son who used to work there. When I said his name was Everett, he said, "OMG, I love Everett," as I secretly burst with mommy pride. "He was just in here a few days ago, and, like, everyone stopped to say hi to him."

I then moved to the place where you wait for your food to be prepped. I started talking to one of the girls after she greeted me. "Hey," I said. "Do you know Everett who used to work here?" She smiled, and said, "Yeah." "I'm his mom," I said. "Seriously? Oh my god, I love him!" she said. I told her I had been banished from coming to this restaurant, but now that he's not here, I can. She immediately texted him that she met me, for the fun of annoying him or eliciting some response.

Just to annoy me, he never mentioned the incident until I asked him about it. I hadn't had a chance to engage with Everett's peers for about three years by then, let alone conspire with them to annoy him. I think this was a prouder mommy moment than his high school graduation. I got a glimpse into who he is in his real life, and he was living it as a fun, friendly, and well-liked person.

6. **He considers you to be a reliable source**

Another great lesson I learned from Alison Armstrong was that men always "consider the source" when it comes to weighing conflicting information. It's a neat little trick. Lord knows my mind has been rattled by people who shouldn't even have been allowed a second thought in my brain.

TEN SIGNS YOU'RE A GOOD MOM

A few years ago, Everett had a conversation with a family-in-law member who had some disparaging remarks to say about me. I was shocked and hurt by them. All he said was, "Mom, consider the source." Problem solved.

7. He shows appreciation

Random acts of appreciation via texting have become my son's method of choice for thanking me out of the blue. My heart wants to burst sometimes when it happens or at least have someone around to show them my phone and say, "Look at what he just said!"

Since no one's around, I've used Facebook a few times instead. This from 2014:

> "Mom, y'know all those times you sat at McDonald's for hours while I played in the playland?"
> "Yep."
> "That was really cool of you."

This from 2015:

> "I'm having a 'pinch me, I must've done something right as a mom' moment. Everett sent me a text around midnight: "I'm watching videos of old Lego sets I had as a kid, and I just wanted to say thank you for all the really nice sets."

And this one from 2018 prior to my book launch:

> I posted that I hoped my book creates a bridge so moms and their adult sons wouldn't have to

keep misunderstanding each other. A few days later, Everett and I were juggling each other's schedules to make some Christmas plans. The day after we figured everything out, he texted:

"I'm glad we understand each other."

8. He takes ownership of something

Fred Miller says that he was surprised that a lot of things that he taught his son actually got through. "I could look at the person, the drug-free person, and the intellectual side of him," says Fred. "I could see the character makeup of the individual. It's one of integrity. I think that he self-consciously wanted to have something to own. What he owns is, 'I do not drink.' I think I showed that it's ok to own something of his own character, and that's more than just a choice or a preference."

Bruce Dane tells a story about Andrew that made him extra proud. When Andrew was younger and staying at his mom's, he snuck out at night. "He and his friends were out running around at a park," says Bruce. "They were out after curfew, and the police came around. It's not a really big deal, right? One of his friends got caught, and everyone else ran off. He went back and turned himself in with his friend. I told him that's the only reason I wasn't going to ground him, because he did the right thing."

Everett owns that he is "straight edge." I had to look up what it means. According to the *Urban Dictionary* it is "someone who respects their body by not consuming alcohol, doing drugs, or having casual sex." His low-key integrity about this is impressive, and Lord knows it's nothing he learned from hanging around certain members of our family.

TEN SIGNS YOU'RE A GOOD MOM

9. **He tells you what you need to hear**

Shortly after the "data minutes" incident, Everett saw me getting dolled up to go greet some arriving guests around eight at night.

"Where are you going?" he said.

"About ten people are arriving. I have to go get them settled in."

"Wait, didn't you just tell me that you haven't been paid for all the work you've done?"

"Well, yeah," I looked down to slip on my shoes. "But I still have to let these people in and show them the place."

"Mom, that is just crazy. You keep doing A+ work all the time, and they don't pay you anything for it. Let them do it."

"Well. Yeah. You're right. But it's not these guests' fault. They still deserve to be welcomed."

"Have you been able to write or anything since you got here?" he said. "Did you write today?"

I rolled my eyes a bit and sighed. "What do you think?"

My son stood up from his desk, and with great passion said, "My God, mom! When are you going to start living your dreams and doing what you want to do instead of sacrificing your life for everyone else?!"

I was like that baby bird teetering in the garage my first day here.

I blinked. I had no answer. He did though.

"Except for me."

10. **He leaves and does well**

The whole job of motherhood is to create your own obsolescence. That means you did it! Applause, applause! While going through the journey of empty nesting, my emotions—as noted herein—got the better of me. I forgot to congratulate or even acknowledge myself for a job well done. So, here's to all the single moms whose sons have flown the coop. Congratulations!

CHAPTER TEN
Take Off

I wish I could write that, by the end of my first year of empty nesting, all my troubles and emotional tsunamis were over. But there were still many kinks to work out, not the least of which was planning our exit to go unscathed and unnoticed by the owners of the Stonecote Estate. Their new tactic was to start charging me to live there now that rentals were fewer for the winter (even though I was still expected to continue to maintain the property and remain as an on-call presence). On the advice of a friend who is a lawyer, it was smart to escape without giving them the heads-up.

Everett was to go first.

Because he had learned the lesson of what having the wrong roommate was like, this time he picked more wisely and had the support of his new roommate's parents. His roommate was a young woman, and they were going to share a two-bedroom apartment in a different part of Louisville that was closer to the colleges. I met her father at the apartment manager's office where we each co-signed for our children. I felt very proud that this father trusted my son to live with his daughter. I also felt relieved and grateful when he offered to pay the entire down payment for the apartment.

It was easier this time around. It felt more grounded in Everett's wants and needs. I was also satisfied by the knowledge that Everett and I had worked through any issues between us, made amends, understood each other better, and completed what we needed to complete.

I had about a month left on the property to pack up my things and move out little by little.

One afternoon while I was in the garage packing boxes, a baby bird flew inside and crashed into one of the far-side windows. I watched with dread as it dropped to the concrete floor behind some boxes.

I moved gently toward where it landed, fearful I might find it injured or dead. To my joy, it was sitting upright and blinking its eyes, but it had no clue what to do next. Just like in the spring, I heard the parents of this little one chirping vociferously in the nearby trees.

I carefully picked it up, cupped it in my hand, and walked out of the garage. I spoke softly to it, saying, "You're ok. You're gonna make it." I opened my palm. That tiny fledgling sat there for at least five minutes; its vulnerability was palpable.

And then, it took off! It found a nearby branch and landed. Its parents flew toward it. Just like me, that bird was getting a second chance to live.

I thought the worst was behind me but then came Christmas. Not only did I have no money to buy presents, I had no Christmas spirit at all. Even worse, when I was going through the process of further purging and packing, I could not find Everett's box full of special ornaments—the ones we or he had selected throughout every Christmas of his life. I felt utter loss and like it was one final blow to my passing mommyhood. To me, our personal family history had disappeared. My heartache resurfaced.

My sister in St. Louis convinced us to come for the holiday. After Everett laid down on the sofa bed to go to sleep that Christmas Eve, Barbara and I started talking. Let me correct that, I started sobbing. I wailed about everything from the lack of gifts to my feelings of failure. "I am nothing. I have nothing. He doesn't need me anymore."

My sister, not being a mother, didn't really know what to say. After a few vain attempts to comfort me, my son popped his head up from the sofa bed.

"Mom, I'm just trying to learn how to be a man," Everett said. "It doesn't mean I don't love you. I just need to be a man. That doesn't make you less."

It was funny that it took a year for us to go through all we went through, and then he just summed up the final result. I stopped crying, thinking *oh yeah, he's becoming a man.*

Light bulb moment. My pity party was over.

NEXT STEPS

Your child was your compass

I think that the needle on any mom's compass points toward the initials of their children's names. My north was E for Everett. My life was more about his life than my own. My pressing life issues were: How can I get him fed while still doing my job? How can I get him to school on time while doing my job? How can I help him with his homework or run his errands and be a good mom while doing my job?

"I didn't prepare myself for this," says Yolandra Drake. "I didn't even know that you could be prepared. You're never going to prepare yourself fully, because you're so busy as a single parent doing things on your own, it's really hard to take the time to do that. You get really dependent on your kids. I had no clue that I should start thinking about those things or what to expect or what to do next."

When you're a single mom, you don't have a spouse or a partner in the house. Yolandra recalls that friends and people in past relationships would say, "'You know, it just seems like you don't have any space for someone else, because you have your routine. You got your life together.' Ok, now I have space. My child was my number one commitment, yes, and someone would've had to come in number two or three, sorry. She's still got that number one space, just not in the house," says Yolanda.

Change your north to you

"Now it's time to focus on what really makes you tick going forward, because so much of your life has always been for them," says Laura Bartlett. "For me, it was a willful choice to compromise whatever my wants or needs were for them. But now, I would encourage moms to really think about switching gears and think about yourself. What is it you want? Where do you want to go? What are your goals?"

You need to take time to process your future plans without having to factor someone else into the picture. Just start there. Make a list of what you want to be, do, and have. Think about anything that you may have delayed, like a long-awaited dream or goal.

"I was already doing a lot of that while my sons still lived with me," says Laura. "I made a transition in my late thirties to start doing standup comedy. I definitely delayed that dream, but I started doing it when they were old enough so that it worked with a shared custody situation when they were at their dad's when I worked. I just started putting myself out there."

Dr. Beth Halbert says that her tips for directing your compass apply before you have children, while you have children, and, *for sure,* before your children leave the nest. "Take divine decadent loving care of yourself. Some people don't even know what that means or what it looks like," Beth says. "I know when I started asking myself questions like, 'What do I want, What do I need, or What are my desires to live into?' I realized a lot of those questions and answers had been snuffed out of my being. It was too painful to think about, because I had what I call the 'super seven-year-old brain' that was telling me I should've already done it, and it should've already happened. The *should* monster kicked in."

Beth says that her most important tip would be to ask yourself, "'What would bring you joy?' I asked the parents of a 14-year-old, 'What would you do if he wasn't in your life? How would you be living life if you didn't have a son that was driving you crazy?' I advised them to do that now." She says to give yourself that gift right now, too.

Many parents hem and haw at the suggestion. I probably would've been one of them, but no one ever suggested it. Beth says that her patients imagined how they'd do this and go do that and be gone for a week and on and on. "I said, 'Ok, so let's find a way to get you a vacation for a week.' Immediately they said they couldn't do that. I said, 'Ok, assuming that really is the truth, I will take that answer even if I don't believe it. But let's take it back to how can you do a day? How can you do a Tuesday? How can you do three hours? What can you do that would bring you bliss and joy, and let's get that list going right now.'"

You were meant to fly

Empty nesting eventually becomes your second chance to do what you want to do. It's your turn to be a woman first instead of a mother first. Making that switch is freeing, but at first quite jarring.

Down the road from the Stonecote Estate, there is a beautiful seminary that stands alongside Cherokee Park. As I walked the property and through the woods while pondering my next steps, I stumbled upon a labyrinth.

A labyrinth is an ancient symbol that relates to wholeness. It's used as a walking meditation or spiritual practice and is arranged so that the participant moves through a series of curves, ending at the labyrinth's heart or center. Walking the labyrinth represents a journey to our own center and then back again out into the world. I must have walked that labyrinth at least ten times during my last month at Stonecote. I do believe that walking that path restored my sense of self and allowed me to surrender to whatever would come. It was the first time in a long time that I was able to explore the possibilities for my new life and my next steps, and to do so without tears.

"You're so busy trying to help them prepare for college and wherever else they may be going and making sure they have everything else they need," says Yolandra. "For me personally, I didn't really have a lot of time to think about myself, and then suddenly it was 'Now, what am I gonna do?' I had all this time on my hands suddenly."

Yolandra's daughter told her she needed to get in a relationship and that she needed love and to find a man. Instead, Yolandra pursued other things. "I'm realizing that I don't have tolerance for a lot of crap, so it's like you just don't want to deal with that. It does get a little lonely, but I just didn't think about it. I got busy. It gave me an opportunity to put my passion into other things, including publishing my book, *Single Parent Secrets*. My daughter was still here with me in spirit, because I was on the phone with her several times a day, every day."

I think that's one of the main differences between empty nesting with a son versus a daughter. Moms and daughters will likely still chat and can become more like girlfriends. Regardless, it's hard when your child leaves. "It's gonna hit you no matter what," says Yolandra. "But once you get up off the floor and start doing something, that's a more valuable way to spend your time."

Revel in your and your adult child's successes

Take time to notice what you accomplished as a mom.

Give yourself a pat on the back.

Yolandra reflects about what it's like to see her daughter, now that she's a young woman and living on her own in her own apartment. "Things are just coming together in her life. That's a great feeling," says Yolandra. "It's like, okay I don't have to worry. She went through so much in college, and I prayed all the time, and God kept saying, 'Don't worry so much, you got this' and 'Just give it time, you've got it.'" Yolandra says that now everything is coming full circle.

"My daughter was my biggest cheerleader all the time. I won many award trips from my company to Hawaii, but she could never go because she was under-age, and they didn't allow kids. I've wanted to include her on one of these trips for all the ways she supported me and helped me win," says Yolandra. "I finally got the opportunity to take her last year before she went away to law school. We went on the president's trip with her as my guest. Being with her as a young adult was so refreshing. It was a wonderful experience to finally share that with her right before she left to do her own thing. She had waited so long to go, and finally, after all that time, I could say, 'You get to come with me. It finally worked out.' It was really, really good."

Fred Miller says there are so many significant things to be proud of about his son. "He went to a Christian school, and he made the choice to get baptized. He made his own decision," says Fred. "Even to this day, he's gone through a lot of different churches, and one of the last conversations I had with him was about his joining another church. Churches are different; it's all about the characters and the people. I don't think he's elevated to the point where he can separate himself from the human aspect of the church, meaning the membership and the parishioners, and just focus more on his objective for when he goes. But he's been able to maintain his sense of spirituality and stay consistent with it. And I really like that about him."

Terri felt her own sense of pride the day her daughter, Kelsey, graduated from high school. "I was super ecstatic for so many reasons. It really is a relief," Terri says. "Especially because, when I was pregnant, people were asking me about adopting her, because they just didn't think I was going to be right to be a parent. It really is a nice feeling when your kids make it all the way through high school, and they're okay and they're safe and they're alive and they're healthy. It's an amazing milestone."

Create new traditions

While packing my belongings, I found Everett's Christmas ornaments—*in the box marked Halloween*! I jumped for joy. Everett and I then created two new traditions for the holidays. One, we'd have Thanksgiving breakfast together instead of dinner. That left us free to have Thanksgiving dinner with our own friends. The second new tradition was to get a smaller Christmas tree and only hang our special ornaments on it. These new traditions helped us own our new life.

Give your children the gift of your own happiness

Your children want you to be happy and to enjoy a life that no longer evolves around them. (Except, as my son would joke, when he needs it to.) Commit to giving yourself back to your own life again and let them commit to theirs. The possibilities are endless.

"I'm a pharmaceutical sales rep and have been doing it for a while now," says Yolandra. "Now, I'm also doing author events and talks. I'm learning a lot about marketing myself as opposed to marketing for my company. It's so much easier to market for someone else."

Terri Kendall, the now-retired high school psychologist, pursued aerials and circus performance arts while her youngest daughter was still in school. In fact, they went to classes and trainings together. She continues to be a sought-after performer and high-level artist as the owner of XaltTalent.com. Since retiring from her psychology career, Terri obtained her real estate license, married her dream man, started a job as an adjunct professor at Bellarmine University, and became a health coach and certified personal trainer.

Laura Bartlett, the executive producer and one of the talented comics in *Four Funny Females,* is now a business partner with her youngest son. Their product, Wine Condoms, is a smashing success. She is also the founder of idonotconsent.com, working to inform patients about dangerous Covid hospital protocols still impacting vulnerable patients and how to protect yourself and your loved ones.

And I finally wrote this book, which won Transformational Author Experience awards in 2015 and 2018. I built a ghostwriting and editing business at authorjoy.com to help new and accomplished authors bring their best books forward. For 12 months I became a nomad in 2020 and 2021 and traveled the American open road. As soon as I discovered the Black Hills of South Dakota I never wanted to leave, and they are now my forever home. Since then I created the Nomad Woman Network to help other solo women travelers experience safety, discovery, and joy on the road at nomanwomannetwork.com.

During my nomad journey, I'd stop in Louisville to visit Everett. It made me so sad to see him wearing a mask over his face, while I intentionally did quite the opposite. One night, as he left my motel room, he stopped and said, "Mom, you are in a Renaissance period." His pride in me meant more than all other achievements combined.

Remember you're always role modeling

My boxes were packed and loaded into the storage unit. I cleaned the carriage house and left 50 bucks on the counter for the girls who cleaned the estate who may come to clean some more. I locked all the doors to the property and left the keys on the counter of the main house. I was ready to say goodbye to this phase of my life, and once again start anew. Everett was there to help with the final packing. My actions were setting an example of how to overcome challenges, though I didn't think about it like that at the time.

"When it comes to our kids, they notice what you do as a parent and your involvement in their lives," Fred says. "They see it. They hear conversations. They look at your mannerisms. They look at your struggles and how you persevere. Someone who perseveres instills that same kind of strength and resilience to handle the adversities of life. It makes them stronger because it's actually the kind of person they will become attracted to. It's like you said with your son, you know you're proud. There were times that things were unstable, you just didn't know, and there were a lot of insecurities. But you know, when you get past that period, you can look at it and say, 'Wow, I did a good job.'"

I turned to look at the beautiful estate one last time.
"Well kid, this is it."
We hugged before getting in our cars.
"Mom," he called out across the driveway.
"Yeah, honey?"
"Drive safely."

Afterword

It's been said that, whatever obstacle or trial you endure, there is an important lesson for you to learn or a payoff to receive that you are painfully unaware of at the time you're going through it.

For me, the payoff for my work at the venue was to come from Amy Eicher, the new owner of Stonecote Estate. I called Amy to introduce myself and ask if I could have my book launch party there. After realizing I was the Lauren mentioned in the reviews on vrbo.com, Amy said, "You're *that* Lauren? Of course you can have your event here, free of charge!"

I was able to meet Pete, the property manager who replaced me. I was happy to hear that Amy began paying him immediately when she and her husband bought the property.

My book party at Stonecote Estate was one of the best nights of my life and another instance of completion. Thank you, Amy Eicher, for affirming there are kind and generous people who enjoy helping others achieve their dreams.

AFTERWORD

"Each step we take in our journey, no matter what the landscape appears to be or feels like, is our place of birthing into more wholeness. We all know, looking back at our lives, of a time when we came to kiss the feet of a difficult experience. Where we came to see the gold within it. Where we came to understand there was a gift there for us."

—Sarah Blondin

Recommended Resources

The Venue

Stonecote Estate, Louisville, Kentucky. The property is still going strong as a 5-star destination as of 2026 with new owners over the years. Check it out at https://www.vrbo.com/561839

Experts

Alison Armstrong has been designing and leading transformational programs for adults for over 30 years. Find out about Alison's innovative programs for men and women at www.alisonarmstrong.com

Andre Paradis is on a mission to bridge the gap between men and women. He is a Relationship Coach, NLP Coach, Workshop Leader, Public Speaker, and a bestselling author. www.projectequinox.net

Lori Finlay is a Nurse Practitioner, Board Certified Health Coach, and Certified Creation Coach. I am the Editor of her bestselling and award-winning book *Create the Vitality You Crave*. www.LoriFinlay.com

RECOMMENDED RESOURCES

Lana M. Kontos, ND helps high-performing professionals and entrepreneurs in the US, Puerto Rico, Canada, and the Bahamas stay on their "A" game without fatigue, a foggy brain, or the weight gain. www.inspiredbywellness.com

Books

I will not die an unlived life: RECLAIMING PURPOSE AND PASSION
By Dawna Markova

Goddesses Never Age
By Christiane Northrup, MD

Why A Son Needs A Mom: 100 Reasons
By Gregory E. Lang

Love You Forever
By Robert Munsch

Creating Sacred Space with Feng Shui
By Karen Kingston

Create the Vitality You Crave: Epigenetics 101 to Unlock Your Healing Power
By Lori Finlay, MSN, NP, CNS, BCC

Hormonal Support

SomaDerm Transdermal Gel to increase natural growth hormone
www.newulife.com

Rowe Casa Organics for Hormone Wellness Drops
www.rowecasaorganics.com

Exercise

Online fitness programs are cheaper and more convenient than a gym with much more variety in classes and trainers. There's something for everyone at www.beachbodyondemand.com

Meditations

The Insight Timer App

Sarah Blondin's *Live Awake* meditation series is what helped me move from breakdowns to breakthroughs. www.sarahblondin.com

Share the love

If you liked what you read and want to help more moms and sons, I'd appreciate your honest review. Thanks a bunch!

IF YOUR STORY'S CALLING YOU TO WRITE— OR WANDER—LET'S CHAT. SCHEDULE YOUR FREE 15-MINUTE STRATEGY SESSION AND BEGIN YOUR NEXT ADVENTURE WITH CLARITY AND LIFT.

authorjoy.com/strategy

www.ingramcontent.com/pod-product-compliance
Lightning Source LLC
Chambersburg PA
CBHW020908080526
44589CB00011B/499